Collaborative Stage Directin

Collaborative Stage Directing: A Guide to Creating and Managing a Positive Theatre Environment focuses on the director's collaboration with actors and the creative team, and the importance of communication and leadership skills to create and manage a healthy working environment. Speaking directly to the student, this compact resource walks the aspiring director through basic principles of group dynamics, active listening, open-ended questioning, brainstorming, and motivational leadership, supported by examples and case studies offered by current professional and academic directors. With a focus on preparing the student director for resume-building opportunities beyond the studio lab, *Collaborative Stage Directing* challenges readers with reflective activities, a series of guiding questions to apply to three short plays, and an extensive checklist to assist them with independent directing projects. As an easy-to-use resource, *Collaborative Stage Directing* works as a supplement to a classic directing text or as a stand-alone guide.

Jean Burgess, PhD is a theatre educator, director, and playwright who taught college-level theatre for over twenty years and has been directing for over forty years. She received an MA in Theatre from Northwestern University and a PhD in Educational Theatre from New York University.

Collaborative Stage Directing

A Guide to Creating and Managing a Positive Theatre Environment

Jean Burgess

Routledge
Taylor & Francis Group

NEW YORK AND LONDON

First published 2019
by Routledge
52 Vanderbilt Avenue, New York, NY 10017

and by Routledge
2 Park Square, Milton Park, Abingdon, Oxon, OX14 4RN

Routledge is an imprint of the Taylor & Francis Group, an informa business

Library of Congress Cataloging-in-Publication Data
A catalog record for this title has been requested

ISBN: 978-0-367-08618-3 (hbk)
ISBN: 978-0-367-08619-0 (pbk)
ISBN: 978-0-429-02340-8 (ebk)

Typeset in Sabon
by Swales & Willis Ltd, Exeter, Devon, UK

MIX
Paper from
responsible sources
FSC
www.fsc.org
FSC™ C013985

Printed in the United Kingdom
by Henry Ling Limited

Contents

Acknowledgments

For diversity of thought and experience, I incorporated a survey questionnaire about the collaborative process and invited several directing colleagues from around the country to participate. My thanks go out to the following friends, colleagues, and former students who agreed to share their experiences and insights on the collaborative process in their own directorial work, whether in the academic, community, or professional arena: Hamilton Clancy, Kate Danley, Donald Hicken, Noah Himmelstein, Dallas Munger, Richard Pilcher, and Elizabeth van den Berg. Your unique approaches to the craft are a gift.

A special thank you is extended to Ira Domser and the students of his Theatre Appreciation class at McDaniel College (Fall 2017). Ira and I collaborated on an Acting and Directing unit for his class, where I was able to workshop the original plays and directing concepts in this text. Thank you, Ira, for your continued support, inspired collaborations, and great friendship through many years.

Throughout the text I relate stories of personal directing and acting experiences I have encountered, and many outstanding teachers, designers, and directors I've had the pleasure to work under, collaborate with, or observe. Of course, a short text such as this limits my use of examples and I in no way mean to snub any of the wonderful teachers, designers, and directors I've been exposed to in my forty-plus years of theatre work as well as the fine theatre organizations that have been a part of my artistic foundation. I'd like to extend particular thanks to my early mentors, some of whom I have specifically mentioned in the guide: Carl Schurr, Gwen Yarnell, Tim Ryan, Mary Pat Daley, Ira Domser, Chris Vine, Maureen O'Neill, The School of Fine Arts (Willoughby, Ohio), Ursuline College (Pepper Pike, Ohio), Northwestern University (Evanston, Illinois), and New York University (New York, New York). Suffice to say, you have all made an impact on the director and theatre professional I am today.

Thank you to my editor, Stacey Walker, and editorial assistant, Lucia Accorsi, at Routledge/Taylor and Francis, who patiently answered all my questions throughout this process.

I would be remiss if I did not extend a giant thank you to my sister, Barbara Burgess Van Aken, for her continued encouragement and editing skills. She has been a constant champion throughout this project, and I am so grateful for her loving support.

Finally, I thank my husband, Don McCombie, for not only making sure my computer behaved at all times, but also for being a willing proof-reader with a keen eye. Thank you, Don, for your constant love and belief in me.

Foreword

What causes anyone to become a director? What are the commonly held beliefs, desires, tastes, temperaments, sensibilities, skill sets? What makes a director effective or even necessary? These questions have arisen for me during my nearly fifty-year-long career as a director and as an educator. In my experience, directors seem to spring from various and varied wells: actors who are tired of being told what to do by people who, they feel, know less than they do; writers (journalists mostly) who want to control how dramatic literature (mostly their own) should be realized on stage; enthusiasts who have connections with producers and a talent for charming theatre professionals into working with them; driven visionaries with a passion for theatre and no other outlet for their inexhaustible energies; dramaturges fascinated with dramatic literature; and folks who simply want to make theatre because it's fun and "interesting" but who can't act and have poor eye-to-hand coordination. Each journey has its own hazards: actors tend to get lost in specifics without a grasp of the big picture; writers' creative force is putting lived experience into words on a page and they seldom possess the sensibilities required to do the reverse; enthusiasts enjoy the prestige but, too often, haven't been required to acquire the skill and experience; driven visionaries struggle with relinquishing control to collaborators; dramaturges understand content but often lack the practical knowledge of what works on stage; and the simple folks who come to directing by the process of elimination are seldom able to find dynamic inspiration. Additionally, most directors tend to be specialists who have an affinity for certain playwrights or genres and too often find themselves required by financial mandates or academic calendars to direct plays for which they feel no affinity. A director with no fire in his/her own belly is likely to be uninspiring and ultimately ineffective.

As Dr. Burgess points out in her premise for writing this book, perhaps the greatest hazard facing the creative process of making theatre is a director who is on a power-trip. If a director is motivated by "being in

charge," "realizing his/her vision," or "bringing something new and exciting to the text," it is quite likely that actors, designers, stage managers,
and even producers will find themselves swimming upstream against the
current of an ego in desperate need of gratification. Gordon Rogoff once
wrote in an essay for *American Theatre* magazine: "American directors
have long since forgone the rigors of the text and the needs of the actors
in favor of smart moments featuring themselves." The keys to effective
directing (which seem to elude many who want to call themselves directors) seem to be humility, curiosity, spontaneity, and the capacity to be a
persistent and effective listener.

So, if the hazards are so many, the requirements for success so rigor-
ous and the personal qualities so lofty, why have a director at all? The
position is, in the grand history of the art of theatre, a rather recent
"requirement." For centuries theatre flourished under the guidance of
a chorepheus or an actor/manager who, while performing a leading
role, provided all the organization necessary for a play to make it to an
audience: casting, interpretation of text, blocking, even the curtain call.
Directors, as we understand them today, are an invention of the late 19th
and early 20th centuries. We got along without them before we met them –
can we get along without them now? Probably not – and why not?
Perhaps it is our need for efficiency (time being money) or perhaps it is
our habit of hierarchy (we need someplace for the buck to stop). But for
whatever reason, directors are here to stay.

The main reason I stopped railing against the director as interloper and
thief of an art form which rightfully belongs to actors is that I see myself
as a surrogate for the one indispensable ingredient which is, by necessity,
missing from the rehearsal process – the audience! In rehearsal I am the
eyes, ears, intellect, and emotions of those who will pay to see what is
created. I am required to stand in for those who will receive and return
the energy coming from the stage – thus making complete this art we call
theatre. My job is to engage all my senses, all my receptors, and my vul-
nerabilities in order to access every moment for its clarity, honesty, and
creative energy. I have to walk the path traveled by each character and
cement that journey (arc) in my consciousness. I must know every nuance
of every relationship in the text and I must be able to judge effectively
how all this is realized moment to moment. I must identify the central
tensions and conflicts through a thorough investigation of why the play
was written in the first place. These processes require that I know what
works on stage, and that takes years to cultivate even if the gift is genuine.
The margin of error is wide and frightening – maybe that's where some
of the excitement lives. I know where I've been wrong when we meet that
first audience and I watch and listen for the responses (even the quality
of the silence). The art is happening in the space shared by actors and
audience, and if that space feels dead, devoid of communication which

can be felt, then I know something essential is missing and needs to be identified and given the requisite energy. I also learn where I needed to be more open, vulnerable and inventive in my role as surrogate audience during the rehearsal process.

The enormous challenge and responsibility assumed by the director cannot be minimized, and should be taken on with diligence, rigor, humility, grace, and respect. This book provides a pathway to effective directing which includes not only the "nuts and bolts," but also the essential mindset. Taken as a guidebook and as a workbook, it will provide the student director (and every good director is always a student) an important creative framework for preparing to enter perhaps the most magical place on the planet – the rehearsal hall.

Donald Hicken
Resident Director, The Annapolis Shakespeare Company
2015 Tony Award Finalist for Excellence in Theatre Education
2001 Helen Hayes Award Winner for Outstanding Director

Preface

This text is not meant to be a directing textbook. There are many wonderful directing texts, which teach students the why and how of directing for the stage. *Collaborative Stage Directing: A Guide to Creating and Managing a Positive Theatre Environment* is meant as a guide to supplement a student director's basic knowledge and experience. Moving from conceptual ideas to guided application to independent application and interspersed with reflective and practical activities, *Collaborative Stage Directing* asks readers to connect to the mindset of being a respectful, motivational and communicative director.

Based on my observation of twenty-three years of college-level theatre teaching, student directors are anxious to "be in charge" of their first directing project, but are often ill-prepared in how to communicate and lead their peers. (I know I certainly was when I was an undergrad directing student!). Often directing courses do little to teach the basic communication and leadership skills that go a long way in establishing an open environment for creativity to flourish. Instead what invariably occurs is that the student director becomes insecure and overcompensates with an authoritative attitude – killing any budding theatrical collaboration. I've seen it over and over. It's not the student directors' fault. They simply do not have the understanding or the tools at their disposal.

Whether directing within the classroom, an independent project, or a first professional production, this guide will become an indispensable resource. My goal is twofold: to help young directors understand why establishing an open creative working environment is essential to theatrical collaboration and therefore the success of their productions, and to provide tools to help directors navigate through the communication and leadership challenges, such as:

How do I create and manage a positive working environment?

How can I promote collaboration to generate creative ideas to problem-solve?

How do I talk to my creative team?

How do I ask the right kind of questions of my actors?

Collaborative Stage Directing: A Guide to Creating and Managing a Positive Theatre Environment is intended for theatre students who are interested in working beyond the technical aspects of directing their independent projects. This guide will push student directors to reflect deeply about their individual approach in communicating with both actors and their creative team, to consider the kind of rehearsals they want to run, and to ask themselves what place leadership and mutual respect have in the theatre. Whether using *Collaborative Stage Directing* as a supplement along with another directing text or as a solo guide, these reflective questions, exercises, examples, and case studies are meant to steer young directors toward success in their directing journey.

Letter to the Instructor

Dear Theatre Educator,

I admire what you do on a daily basis. I can say this with great under-standing, because I was a theatre educator for twenty-three years. What I observed in many academic theatre settings was one of two scenarios – either a formal directing class was offered, or more likely, a handful of students were permitted to direct independent projects with little instruc-tion. In the formal class situation, which is ideal in my opinion, the students received instruction and classroom application before embark-ing on independent directing projects. In the second example, the students were more or less set free with very little guidance outside of the occa-sional rehearsal check-in by an overworked instructor to make sure the project wasn't an utter disaster.

I also repeatedly observed a misunderstanding among student direc-tors about the role of the director, especially as it relates to directing their peers. This misunderstanding was so intense and destructive to the spirit of directing that I feel it needs to be addressed. If we can help young directors avoid this misunderstanding from the onset, together we will go a long way in helping them develop as successful directors. What is this colossal misunderstanding? That somehow a director is the boss of the production. Other words can be interjected: "head," "dictator," or "grand master." I once walked past the rehearsal studio and overheard a student director yelling at her cast, "This is *my* show and you're making me look bad." Clearly this misunderstanding was learned somewhere along the line.

My belief is that collaboration based on excellent communication and leadership skills is the key to directing success. What I set out to do is to create a reference guide for instructors to use in the formal directing class setting, and for directing students to use during independent projects.

I want to not only dispel this misunderstanding among young directors, but also provide information on how to create a positive working environment as well as helpful management tools to use during independent directing projects.

You may be asking yourselves: Do we really need another directing text for student directors? If you're like me, your office bookshelf holds a wide range of classic authors on directing from Harold Clurman to William Ball to Francis Hodge to Alexander Dean and Lawrence Carra. As I canvassed numerous theatre faculty while writing this book, I heard over and over that they can't find one single directing text that satisfies all their needs. They tend to use bits and pieces from a variety of texts, including these classics. I agree with their assessment. Our directing students still need some of the technical instruction provided in texts similar to *Fundamentals of Play Directing* by Alexander Dean and Lawrence Carra, while they also need to understand how a director analyzes the play and deals with each phase of the production, which is handled beautifully in Michael Bloom's *Thinking Like a Director* and Robert Knopf's *The Director as Collaborator*.

Collaborative Stage Directing: A Guide to Creating and Managing a Positive Theatre Environment focuses primarily on directing as collaboration with actors and the creative team, and the importance of communication and leadership skills – unique tools not often provided in our classic directing literature. This guide is meant to supplement any of these excellent texts, whichever you may choose. Additionally, it is the perfect stand-alone guide for student directors working on independent projects to remind and encourage them to use collaborative practices.

Blending personal stories of successes and failures with surveys and interviews with current professional theatre directors from venues across the United States, I've created a backdrop for students to envision their next career steps. While all may hope for an assistant directing slot at The Guthrie or The Shakespeare Theatre, many directing students will be building a resume by accepting directing jobs at a non-Equity New Play Festival, a local community theatre, a summer stock, or a Theatre for Young Audiences venue. With this reality in mind, this guide is filled with examples of collaboration in a variety of those settings.

Additionally, to enhance the reader's personal growth, the guide offers chapter reflections and activities, application exercises associated with three short plays, and a broad list of guiding questions in the form of a checklist to apply to the student director's own directing projects. I have incorporated three original short plays for the following reasons:

1   Many college theatre programs as well as professional theatre companies include New Play festivals or programs in their seasons. This is a trend in which young directors can find entry opportunities. Therefore, it requires young directors to be able to approach directing projects with no preconceived ideas or contextual information about the piece.
2   Ten-minute plays give a sense of completeness that often a long scene cannot. In providing a beginning/middle/end, plot exposition, character development, plot twist, and a quick denouement, the young director finds the challenge to create from square one.
3   As a directing teaching tool, the ten-minute play demands the same amount of preparation and communication a longer play may require, but has the great advantage of less strain on resources and shorter rehearsal time.
4   The three original plays in this guide are meant as training exercises. By applying the guiding questions, the student directors are receiving valuable practice in preparation for both the New Plays trend as well as more traditional directing projects.

By design the guide moves the student from concept to guided application to independent application, and includes activities for self-reflection and journal work throughout, with the goal of guiding students toward individualized growth. Online journaling is an efficient way for the instructor to check in directly with students while they work through the application activities, and, during their independent directing projects, red-flag any potential problems before a crisis occurs without having to attend every rehearsal. Additionally, this historical record will become invaluable as students' skills develop and experiences expand.

You will notice that much of the guide references Western theatre practices and conventional theatre environments such as proscenium, thrust, or Theatre-in-the-Round staging. This is not to discourage the exploration of environmental staging, devised or interactive theatre, puppet or shadow theatre, dance theatre, or so many other exciting, culturally diverse approaches to productions. Rather, the focus of this guide is mastery of the basics – the collaborative skills needed to create and manage a positive theatre environment for the young directors' creative team and actors. Once mastered, they will expand their repertoire with confidence.

Finally, it is my hope that together we can guide young student directors to dispel any misunderstanding about what it means to be a director, to begin to master communication and leadership skills as they create and manage positive working environments, and to become the very best theatre collaborators they can possibly be. Thank you for all you do every day as a theatre educator.

Yours in education,
Jean Burgess, PhD

Letter to the Student Director

Dear Student,

Congratulations! You've been assigned your first big directing project and you're looking for some guidance on how to manage your creative team. Or perhaps you're preparing for one of many student directing projects, but this time you've decided to approach the rehearsal process a little differently. Or maybe, based on past unpleasant directing experiences, you've found yourself asking: Is there a better way? Whatever your reason for seeking different directorial points of view early in your career, I applaud your initiative. *Collaborative Stage Directing: A Guide to Creating and Managing a Positive Theatre Environment* will discuss several strategies that can be useful to you in your production preparation, pre-production meetings, and rehearsal process – now and in the next steps of your directing career.

The best place to start is with you, the director, and your understanding of the collaborative process. So often with new directors, there is a misunderstanding about the power of the director. Unfortunately, many young directors take the idea of "ruling with an iron fist" to the extreme. They allow their ego to interfere, often building a stifling environment where very little creativity can flow. On the other hand, newer directors may not want to make waves, coming into rehearsal with no prepared concept, allowing the actors to change ideas on a whim, and permitting the creative team to run amok.

You need to create a happy medium. It is the director's job to set the tone and create the collaborative working environment from day one. How will you accomplish this? By incorporating great communication and leadership skills along with an expansive knowledge of theatre arts. Chapter 1 focuses on the many broad skills a director needs. Chapter 2 defines the elements and advantages of creating a positive environment for collaboration. Chapter 3 delves into four main communication strategies you can use to manage that environment: Group Dynamics, Brainstorming, Active Listening, and Questioning skills. A number of exercises, warmup activities and improvisation suggestions are also provided. The detailed case study in Chapter 4 illustrates the way these directorial principles and skills synthesize in an actual production of *I Never Saw Another Butterfly* by Celeste Raspanti. Chapters 5–10 include three short plays and ask you to apply specific guiding questions in the Preparation, Pre-Production and Rehearsal Phases of directing. These application activities require thoughtful, reflective work and stretch your in-depth directorial training. Finally, Chapter 11 provides a broad list of guiding questions in the form of a checklist to apply to your next independent directing project, while Chapter 12 summarizes with concluding thoughts.

You will notice that much of the guide references Western theatre practices and conventional theatre environments such as proscenium, thrust, or Theatre-in-the-Round staging. This is not to discourage the exploration of environmental staging, devised or interactive theatre, puppet or shadow theatre, dance theatre, or so many other exciting, culturally diverse approaches to productions. Rather, the focus of this guide is mastery of the basics – the collaborative skills needed to create and manage a positive theatre environment for your creative team and actors. Once mastered, you will expand your repertoire with confidence.

The guide blends personal stories of both successes and failures with surveys and interviews with current professional theatre directors from venues across the United States in an effort to give you an idea of the multiple avenues available for resume-building. While it would be ideal to step into a regional theatre directing position, be aware that many opportunities to expand your craft can be found at local non-Equity theatres, summer stocks, Theatre for Young Audience venues, community theatres, or New Play Festivals. In fact, the New Play trend in both college programs and professional theatres is one of the reasons for including three original short plays for exercise work in this guide. This trend not only creates directing opportunities, but also requires young directors to be able to approach the material with no preconceived ideas or contextual information. The plays in this guide are meant as exercises to help you practice those skills.

Whether your future desire is to direct professionally, teach and direct in an academic setting, or become a community theatre director, the goal is the same – to facilitate the most inspired version of your creative vision as possible and relate to your audience. By earning the respect of both your actors and creative team, you will succeed by collaborating rather than dictating. As a result, you will have created an environment where creativity will flourish.

I wish you every success in your collaborative theatre adventures.
Jean Burgess, PhD

Part I

The Collaborative Theatre Environment

Introduction

What are the qualities that define a good director? Do you feel these qualities can evolve over time, or must a person be born with them, like a genius musician or portrait artist? Chapter 1, "The Director's Challenge," outlines the many skills you need to be a successful director by breaking down your directing projects into phases. Chapter 2, "Creating a Positive Environment for Theatre Collaboration," answers the question: What does a positive working environment look like? Chapter 3, "Managing the Collaborative Theatre Environment," provides specific communication and leadership tools to aid the director. Finally, Chapter 4, "Synthesizing the Principles: A Case Study," applies all of the previously discussed concepts and skills to a production.

Chapter 1

The Director's Challenge

Award-winning director and playwright Michael Bloom was asked by a friend whether he should pursue a directing career. Bloom asked his friend in response:

> Do you have an appreciation for narrative . . . an instinct for staging, a strong visual imagination, an innate musicality, a critical facility, a background in theater history, and an ability to take the heat, ride the lows, and keep a level head around praise and criticism?[1]

Bloom suggests that a person interested in a career in directing should naturally possess these qualities. While this list may seem overwhelming at first glance, break down each component of the list and it speaks volumes. As a director, you already possess an appreciation of the text and most likely find yourself pulled toward certain genres. You probably already have a natural ability to stage moments and visualize the play uniquely, or you wouldn't be attracted to this craft. Feeling a play's rhythms/hearing its tonality may be a developing sense for you. Interestingly, several of Bloom's descriptors deal with keeping the temperament and ego in check. This is an area where growth can be take place, and where communication and leadership skills can be of great benefit.

As a college instructor for many years, students approached me each semester requesting sponsorship of an independent directing project. These were smart, talented theatre students, but most were ill-prepared for such a project. First, these students had rarely bothered to take a formal directing course, and therefore were devoid of any technical directing skills like understanding blocking for clarity of character objective or composition, or how to create rhythm and pacing (for a review of these basics, see Dean and Carra's *Fundamentals of Play Directing* in Appendix E, "Building Your Library/Suggested Reading"). However, even the most technical, by-the-book director can overlook vital components – essential ingredients that can make the difference between a mediocre and an outstanding director.

While Bloom's criteria may feel overwhelming for a student director just starting out, we must start somewhere. However, many haven't given a thought to the many facets of the director's role. There is more to the job than simply telling actors what to do, or the joy of hearing applause when the curtain closes. Let's breakdown the directorial skills you'll need to begin to hone as you take on the role of director.

Directorial Skills

The role of director involves a variety of active skills. As a director, you will find yourself coordinating, delegating, guiding, advising, empowering, participating, and managing in order to ultimately collaborate. The trick is knowing when to incorporate and how to balance each skill. For instance, a strong director will have read and analyzed the play thoroughly for aesthetic, historical, and cultural elements, in addition to having researched and developed a concept prior to the first pre-production meeting, and will be prepared to communicate this concept to the creative team and eventually to the cast. You *coordinate* people, resources, schedules, and contracts as appropriate for the theatre environment in which you are working. You *delegate* tasks and responsibilities to your immediate staff, where appropriate. You *guide* both your creative team and cast by presenting ideas about your vision for the production, while letting them know you are available to *advise* at any time. You explore ways to *empower* your creative team and cast with confidence in their creativity and ability. You *participate* in discussions with an open mind as your creative team present their design ideas and your cast offer feedback. As you can see, these directorial skills set the stage for a collaborative environment without having to assert much control. That's not to say that, at some point, the director may not have to exert some *managing* skills to guide the creative team or actors back on track, should they stray. The constant challenge is balancing the right amount of empowering, guiding, and advising against your urge to overly coordinate, delegate, and manage – keeping in mind the ultimate goal of a collaborative experience and encouraging all participants to fully contribute and grow in the process.

The truth is, when I was a very young director, I did not subscribe to this idea of theatre collaboration. I was too insecure with my own directorial skills, therefore I overcompensated by becoming the ultimate control freak. I over-planned for every rehearsal, blocked and scored every scene in my director's script which I dictated to the actors like a drill sergeant, and left little room for any designers to elaborate on my production concept. As a result, although my early plays always opened with few technical issues, they seemed flat and certainly over-rehearsed. Additionally, I'm not sure my actors and creative team enjoyed the process very much.

I hadn't learned how powerful and inspirational theatre collaboration with my actors and my creative team could truly be. It would take me several years before I learned the balance between a director-led show and a process-driven, collaborative production. As a director, you can still have an overall concept and artistic vision for your show, create a collaborative environment, and see the concept realized by merging good communication and leadership skills with directorial skills. Let's review exactly how those directorial skills are put to use during a directing project.

Coordinating may include (depending on whether you are working in a professional, academic, or amateur theatre environment) securing the rights to the play, paying royalties, determining the dates and times for auditions, securing a location for auditions, choosing a production creative team, creating a rehearsal schedule, securing a location for rehearsals, and scheduling production meetings. In the professional theatre, a producer, production coordinator, or stage manager assume many of these tasks. However, in some academic or amateur venues, the director may be coordinating these efforts. Additionally, an academic or community theatre director may need to coordinate with specialty designers or consultants for the sake of the production. For example, I directed a college production of *A Thousand Cranes*, a Japanese play based on the book *Sadako and the 1000 Cranes*. My aesthetic and cultural production concept required the design work of a professional mask maker, a mural painter, and a Japanese consultant. I coordinated grant writing activities to fund the mask maker, scheduled time for each of these professionals to work with the creative team, and found ways to utilize their unique talents with the cast.

Delegating includes discussing duties and expectations with your assistant director or instructing your dramaturg (if there is one) on research that would be helpful for rehearsals/production meetings. For example, in the academic environment or when working with teens, I prefer to task my student/teen stage manager with any and all communication with the cast and production team on matters of schedules and times, so that I can focus on the creative matters. While professional stage managers have a clear understanding of their job responsibilities, I find that in the non-professional environment it is important to have these expectations articulated early in the process to avoid misunderstandings.

Guiding includes communicating your concept/vision to the actors and creative team via keywords, photographs, illustrations, artwork, music, and objects. Guiding often requires ingenuity. One of the directors I surveyed for this guide, Dallas Munger of The Chalkboard Players in California, prefers to use audio-visual clips as a reference point for concept conversations with his cast and creative team. In this case, it's about whatever media works best to guide your vision to actualization.

Advising is about making yourself accessible to members of your team should they have questions, concerns, or problems during the process. With the use of texting and email, this can be as simple as a quick design question answered promptly, or a request for a more extensive meeting when necessary. Accessibility is key here, as it demonstrates your desire for open communication.

Empowering allows the actors to explore the script during the rehearsal process via experimentation, exercises, theatre games, and improvisation, and encourages the creative team to explore your initial concept and present sketches, ideas, and found sound effects, etc. The beauty of empowerment is that it enables the teams to shore up areas in which you may have less experience. Independent West Coast director, playwright and author Kate Danley reinforced this point when she shared:

> I think it is very important as an artist to know your weaknesses and where you need to relinquish control. The wonderful thing about this collaborative art form is that there are geniuses who are really, really great when it comes to sets, lights, costumes, and sound design.

Participating involves jumping in alongside the team. For example, within certain rehearsals, it may be appropriate or even necessary for you to become involved in the exercises or improvisations. I was staging the opera *Carmen* for a summer college music festival at Carroll Community College in Westminster, Maryland. While the lead characters were professional opera singers, several of the chorus members were great singers, but novices to the stage. One particular tavern scene, where the chorus should have been dancing, swaying, and swinging their mugs, was falling flat. After several starts and stops, I jumped up on stage and began dancing and mingling freely with the very shocked chorus members. I'm not a fan of giving line-readings or demonstrating how an actor should act by any means, but occasionally participating in a warmup exercise, an improvisation, or even a moment on stage can be beneficial. In this instance, the *Carmen* chorus loosened up immensely in that tavern scene.

Managing can involve keeping your actors and designers on the path toward realizing your artistic concept for the production. At times, you will need to put on your decision-maker hat in order to reign in a set designer who may be veering too far astray from your original production concept, or actors who are, for example, taking the characterizations into a slapstick stylization rather than doing the headwork to create an honest backstory. At other times, managing means intervening if bad rehearsal habits begin to form. Managing may take the form of approving the final versions of costumes, props, makeup, and hair or wig styles during tech week. This is where your job as director can become challenging. Remember, balance is your constant goal.

Some directors might argue that they incorporate other skills in their process. In fact, renowned director and theatre critic Harold Clurman has been known to say the job consists of being "an organizer, a teacher, a politician, a psychic detective, a lay analyst, a technician, a creative being . . . . All of which means he must be a great lover."[2] Additionally, a director must be an excellent leader and communicator, and those skills are the primary focus of this guide.

How will you establish yourself as the leader of your production without coming off as overbearing? How will you pave the way for creativity and inspiration? When asked how professional director and actor Kate Danley balances leadership and collaboration with her creative team and actors during directing projects, she responded:

> You are the leader and your work ethic will set the bar. I believe the best way to lead is to be of service to those around you, so honor and respect the craft and talent others bring to the table. Praise those who are doing well, and address the issues that arise calmly, fairly, and swiftly.

For those of you who have acted onstage, you must admit that you feel more engaged and inspired when you feel respected by your director, when you feel that the environment is fair and encouraging, and when creativity is supported, right?

When we think of a strong leader, what are some of the characteristics that come to mind? Courageous, motivational, disciplined, respectful, fair, adaptable, egoless, and mindful. These are similar to the characteristics that apply to an effective director. In the following section, you will begin to see how the seven directorial skills (coordinating, delegating, guiding, advising, empowering, participating, and managing) as well as communication and leadership skills work together as you progress through the phases of a directing project.

Three Phases of a Directing Project

While it may seem overwhelming, you will be employing every one of these seven directorial skills as you progress through the each phase of your directing project. Personally, I divide my directing projects into three phases, each containing important steps, as shown in Table 1.1. The Preparation Phase includes initial exploration and planning/scheduling. The Pre-Production Phase includes pre-production meetings with your creative team as well as casting/auditions. The Rehearsal Phase includes table readings, blocking, and refining rehearsals, as well as tech week. Each phase demands a focused approach from the production's director. The truth is, I've seen a lot of skimping from young directors, with

Table 1.1 Three phases of a production

Preparation Phase	Pre-Production Phase	Rehearsal Phase
Initial exploration	Pre-production meetings	Early rehearsals
Planning/scheduling	Casting/auditions	Blocking
		Refining rehearsals
		Tech week

plenty of excuses to support their lackadaisical methods. Most just want to get to the actual directing without doing any of the aesthetic, historical, or cultural script analysis. Prep work about the play's setting or time period, creating an overall concept or guiding vision, and even planning a rehearsal schedule is essential. These directors claim they do better by just winging it. Ignoring these preparation practices show little respect for either the creative team or the actors, and the productions generally lack depth.

One of the best approaches you can adopt as a director is a commitment of respect for everyone in your production, and one way to begin to demonstrate that respect is to be prepared. By understanding and utilizing each phase of the directing project to its fullest, you will be very well prepared. Let's briefly review each of the three phases and the associated directorial tasks.

Phase I: Preparation

Initial Exploration

Assuming you have read the play several times, examined its aesthetic/ historical/cultural aspects, considered how these relate to today's audience, and taken notes and jotted down any questions you may have, the initial exploration is the time for researching information about the play and developing the central concept. Your research can include information about the playwright and other works by the playwright, about the play itself, reviews and critical work, and information about the production history of the play and its historical context. Your goals in reading everything written by the playwright are: (1) to learn the rhythm of the playwright's language, (2) to look for repetitive symbolism and themes, and (3) to search for the playwright's social attitudes and personal values. All this information will help you get to the heart and soul of the playwright's intent in the play you are directing.

Another type of research is field work. While it may not be practical in all cases, the use of personal interviews, a visit to a museum, or a trip to an actual location mentioned in the play to gather further information on historical content or visual inspiration can be highly impactful. When directing a play about Japanese culture for a community college, I visited the local art museum for inspiration. Leslie Oden, Jr., who won a Tony Award for his role as Aaron Burr in *Hamilton* on Broadway, visited the Museum of American Finance on a research trip with writer/producer Lin-Manuel Miranda.[3] When field research is not practical, the internet and libraries are viable sources for aesthetic, historical and cultural background work, and inspiration.

An interesting exploration method used by William Ball, famed New York director and founder of the American Conservatory Theatre, is Mental Movie, where after multiple readings of the play, a moving mental image takes form in the director's imagination.[4] This helps the director visualize the play as a whole. I encourage you to experiment with several approaches to your initial play reading/analysis and see what works best for your style. In addition, there are several excellent texts describing the play analysis process in depth, in particular *The Director's Craft: A Handbook for the Theatre* by Katie Mitchell, *The Director as Collaborator* by Robert Knopf, and *Thinking Like a Director: A Practical Handbook* by Michael Bloom (for complete details, see Appendix E). You will be applying one style of play analysis in the practical application portion of this guide in Chapter 6.

The second step in the initial exploration phase is the development of a central concept for the production or what Harold Clurman refers to as the spine[5] (also referred to as vision or metaphor). Directors have their own method for approaching the text and tuning in to the central concept. For example, Donald Hicken, Resident Director of The Annapolis Shakespeare Theatre in Maryland and former Theatre Head of The Baltimore School of the Arts, describes his process as determining "the central energies in the writing (why the play was written, character journeys, and central organizing tension), actor/audience relationship, location and the special demands of the action." Notably, Associate Artistic Director of Everyman Theatre in Baltimore Noah Himmelstein cautions against *imposing* a concept onto a work and warns: "Concept often suggests laying something on top of the work; while I have done this before, I prefer working and lifting from what's there . . . ." Yet another example of concept development is that of Richard Pilcher, Principal Acting Teacher at Baltimore School for the Arts, who describes his process:

> I boil the action of the play down to a single sentence, such as "Looking for justice" or "Trying to fit in." . . . There may be times it oversimplifies the play a bit, but on the whole it's useful to get everyone thinking in a similar way. In addition, I may have a key sentence or so for the overall "image" or feeling of the play. For *Hamlet*, it was the image of a shark swimming through a school of

brightly colored fish – a dark, dangerous presence in the midst of a party. For another show, it was the idea that "nothing is what it seems." I articulate this to the designers well in advance, and to the actors at the first read-through.

It is interesting to note that all three of the directors mentioned above referred to Harold Clurman's legendary text *On Directing*. I highly recommend this book to the serious directing student (see Appendix E).

Many directing texts offer student directors insights on how to approach the development of a concept or central metaphor for a play – defining the "central energies" of the script that speak to you while staying true to the playwright's intent. *A Sense of Direction: Some Observations on the Art of Directing* author David Ball devotes a chapter to exploring the world of the play and metaphor, which he entitles "The Cornerstones for Success." He feels that the discipline of "conforming to one metaphor tends to give the production visual unity, consistency, and power."[6] In *Directing for the Theatre*, authors Sievers, Stiver, and Kahan recommend articulating the concept in a single sentence, such as "This is a play about . . . ."[7] Using the term "approach" rather than concept or vision, Michael Bloom devotes an entire chapter, "Developing the Approach," in his *Thinking Like a Director: A Practical Handbook*. He offers:

> Because directors often get buried in the details of the design and rehearsal process, the approach should function as a goal and a guide through the thicket of moment-to-moment decision-making. It reminds the creative team of the reasons for doing the play in the first place and its significance to a contemporary audience. A resonant approach conveys, whether overtly or subtly, why the play is being produced at that time.[8]

A single word or image, an action phrase, a descriptive sentence – which method of concept development will work best for you? Or will the process change depending on the nature of the play you are directing? I encourage you to begin to experiment with the concept process, even with short directing projects or staged play readings. Research how other directors approach the process and see if their methods work for you. In addition, I have included three approaches for you to consider in Appendix A, "Developing a Production Concept."

Regardless of how you develop your concept, once identified: (1) consider how you will communicate your vision for the production to your creative staff and actors and (2) think about your methods of collaboration. Remember, you are communicating your aesthetic vision, which is often abstract, to a group of creative designers and actors who are eager to be led, inspired, sparked. They want to be included in the process. Consider the language you use, the way you introduce your thoughts and present your research. What works best for me is to create a notebook of my researched information, photos, and clippings, references to music, phrases/words/symbols, and anything else that will help solidify my concept at this point in the process. Any or all of these items may come in handy when presenting your concept to your team to help make the abstract more concrete. More importantly, the way you present this information will determine if you are open to dialogue from your creative team and actors, or if you are closed off to new ideas.

There is one more assumption that must be mentioned at this point in the directorial phases. It is assumed that you love the play you've chosen to direct. Or at the very least, you've chosen a play that intrigues you, challenges you, enthralls you, provokes you, or stimulates you. Early in your directing career, you may be tempted to jump at any paying gig, simply to get a resume credit, even if the pre-determined play is not in your interest area. However, it is very difficult to fake enthusiasm for a project throughout the pre-production and rehearsal stages, and completely unfair to your creative team and cast. As resident director of The Annapolis Shakespeare Company Donald Hicken points out in the Foreword to this guide: "A director with no fire in his/her belly is likely to be uninspiring and ultimately ineffective." Commit to the play that sparks your imagination, energizes your mind, and resonates in your heart.

Planning/Scheduling

Securing the rights to the play, paying licensing and royalty fees, and ordering scripts are tasks that generally fall to the producer or production coordinator. In the professional environment and even most community theatre venues, you would be hired after the play's rights had been secured, freeing you to dive into your initial play analysis and exploration. However, in the academic environment and even some amateur settings, the director may be responsible for securing rights, paying for royalties/licensing fees, and ordering scripts. If you find yourself in this situation, make sure you have a signed contract before you begin your initial exploration, planning, or rehearsal scheduling. You certainly don't want to put time and energy into research and planning only to find out that the play is unavailable!

If, as a director, you need to obtain the rights to a play you wish to direct, the following guidelines may be helpful:

1 Determine which publishing house holds the rights to the play. Each publisher has a catalogue or a website with royalty fees listed. For example, both Samuel French and Dramatist Play Service, Inc. have online application and payment services. Note that fees vary depending

on the producing organization, so make sure you navigate to the correct area on the website (e.g. non-professional or professional/academic or community theatre, etc.)

2 The application is a request for a royalty quote. You will be asked to provide the following information: play title, name of your organization, place of your organization (city, state), seating capacity, ticket prices, non-profit or for-profit status, number of performances, performance dates, Equity or non-Equity.

3 Understand that sometimes plays are "restricted" for various reasons. This may be indicated if you are using a play service online. If you aren't sure, call the publishing house directly to confirm that the play is available for production.

4 You will receive a quote for the royalty fee and a contract or an invoice along with a deadline for payment. Note that plays have different due dates than musicals and each play service company works differently, so read the fine print.

5 Cost of scripts is extra, but they can be ordered directly from the publishing house.

Once you know that the rights are secure for the play, you can begin to prepare your production schedule. This is often done in collaboration with your stage manager or production coordinator. Working backward from your show opening, prepare your rehearsal schedule. If you are considering a musical production, you need to factor in additional time to coordinate both dance and vocal rehearsals as well as blending these into book scenes, and tech rehearsals involving layering in the orchestra. Be sure to include extra rehearsal time for any physical necessities, such as scenes with physical intimacy, fight scenes, or chase scenes. Part of your planning for these physical scenes should include safety considerations and an honest assessment of your own capabilities. For instance, a simple stage slap may be something you have been trained to handle; a stage fist fight needs a professional stage combat consultant. For the safety and respect of your cast, always opt for the consultant. This is an example of demonstrating leadership – knowing when to bring in an expert and delegate responsibilities.

The question of how many hours/weeks of rehearsals to plan for a ninety-minute or two-and-a-half-hour play surfaces quite often. When you are hired by a theatre organization (a community theatre or a teen summer camp or an academic organization), you often are given the parameters of the rehearsal schedule and you simply work within the provided framework. When hired to stage the opera *Carmen* with a combination of professional and non-professional singers, I was given three weeks of evening rehearsals to stage this five-act opera. Generally, in my experience in academic theatre, for productions of a two-hour play, I prefer three-hour rehearsals, four to five evenings a week for five to six weeks before tech week. However, please note that other factors that may influence the rehearsal timetable. Working with inexperienced actors versus seasoned professionals, or intricate stage business/movement versus less complex blocking requirements are examples. You may have to consider the time of year in case weather may cause rehearsal cancellations in your geographical area. I like to start with a rehearsal schedule with extra time built in with the thought that I can scale back if necessary. Generally, directors develop their own workflow preferences after time and experience.

Phase II: Pre-Production

Pre-Production Meetings

Prior to auditions and rehearsals is the time to meet with your creative team (set designer, costumer, light designer, sound designer, props designer, special effects designer, production coordinator, and stage manager) to share your initial concept ideas and get feedback. It is essential that you have completed your research and formulated your concept at this phase so that you present a clear and concise vision to your creative team. At the first meeting, you want to share your thoughts about the play in an open and inviting way, perhaps sharing your research about the playwright in general terms and introducing your concept for the play. Your goal is to empower and unleash these creative minds and imaginations, not to dictate and squash their impulses. If you are working in a professional or larger academic theatre environment, subsequent meetings with your designers will already be scheduled on the production calendar created by a production coordinator, producer, or department head. However, if you've been hired by a community theatre or some other venue where the director is spearheading both the creative team and the acting ensemble, it may be a good idea to ask for a second production meeting a week later with rough sketches (not fully produced, colored renderings that indicate the designers have already made up their minds!) so that discussion and collaboration can continue. Professional resident director Donald Hicken shares a great reminder about priorities in describing his process with production designers: "I listen to designers and tend to respect their visions. I insist that they stick to the story and accept the basic approach . . . . I want clarity. We are working to support the actors."

Casting

Auditions can vary depending on the size of the production, the talent pool, or the type of production. You may decide to hold initial auditions and a callback audition, or simply cast from the initial auditions.

Some directors like to ask actors to come to auditions with a prepared monologue, others prefer to have sides (scenes) prepared from the play, and others will add some improvisation or theatre games. Dallas Munger, founding director of The Chalkboard Players, asks actors to prepare a funny short story about themselves that they can tell in mono-logue form. He finds that it not only allows him to see how well they communicate with the audience, but it also helps him get to know a bit about the actor personally before working together. By contrast, teacher/director Richard Pilcher generally uses a traditional approach to casting through either monologues or scenes. While he has a clear idea of the type of actors he is searching for to fill the character roles from the start, he is prepared to let that notion change if an actor brings something unexpected to the audition. Regardless of the audition approach you choose, you will want to be somewhat flexible in your expectations. You may be delightfully surprised.

What will you look for when casting your play? Over time I developed my own guidelines for assessing an actor during auditions based on five categories: (1) experience of the actor, (2) appropriateness for the role, (3) vocal quality, (4) demonstration of imagination and flexibility, and (5) stage presence. Using a 1–5 rating scale on the audition sheets to indi-cate how the auditionee fares in each category, this system saves me time when there is a large turnout for an audition. However, each project is unique and each role has different requirements. I may select an inexpe-rienced actor who demonstrates great imagination if that is what the role requires. Casting is the first step to a successful production.

Here's what my particular casting assessment looks like in an actual audition. After the stage manager hands me the auditionee's audition form or resume, I quickly jot down abbreviations for my five catego-ries: EX for experience of the actor, A for appropriateness, V for vocal quality, I for imagination, SP for stage presence. After a quick review of the audition form or resume as well as a couple of verbal questions to confirm experience and connect to the auditionee, I jot down a rating of 5 (very experienced), 4 (somewhat experienced), 3 (average experience), 2 (very little experience), or 1 (not much experience). As the audition continues, I continue to use this system for each category, adding adjec-tives about a unique quality in the actor's voice or perhaps something imaginative that occurred in the actor's audition or a strong demonstra-tion of flexibility the actor showed when I asked for an adjustment in the reading. This rating system is entirely subjective, of course, and based on my casting needs for the specific production. Finally, I will jot down a couple of roles that I feel might work for this actor in the upper right-hand corner of the audition form, if applicable.

An alternative and in-depth casting procedure is provided in Dean and Carra's *Fundamentals of Play Directing*, which lists (1) physical appearance,

(2) age, (3) voice quality and diction, (4) sense of movement and rhythm, (5) sense of theatre and background, (6) sensitivity and imagination, (7) audience appeal and power of projection, (8) acting experience, (9) personal tonality, and (10) playing ability for kind and style of play.[9] As you gain directing experience, you will determine which methods and criterion are most important during auditions, and will develop your own guiding principles for casting.

Phase III: Rehearsals

The rehearsal period can extend for weeks, as described earlier, or months depending on the genre of the play or the type of theatre. I've worked in Equity summer stock theatres that produce a new show every two weeks, and college theatres that spend three months developing a Shakespeare production. Generally, the process for a non-musical play begins with early rehearsals including a table read, then moves to blocking, refining rehearsals with actors off-book and working scenes, and finally tech and dress rehearsals. However, each play demands its own approach and each production grows organically. It's best not to be too rigid with the rehearsal process.

Early Rehearsals

During the initial rehearsal, you gather your actors for the first cast meeting and table read – an opportunity for the cast to begin to familiarize themselves with the play and to ask questions. There are two schools of thought regarding the table work. William Ball describes his process in *A Sense of Direction*: "I prefer at least three or four days reading for sense, asking questions about the off stage life of the characters . . .," and he includes confirming entrances and exits, and even correcting pronunciation of words.[10] On the other hand, Donald Hicken offers: "I don't do much table work, preferring to get the actors on their feet and discussing moments when they occur." As you gain experience, you may decide that certain projects will dictate a single read-through, and others will demand more readings and discussion. The choice is up to you.

During the table read, you may want to introduce a tool for actors in character development. In the professional theatre, actors will explore their characters' backgrounds on their own time, using their own methods. However, if you are working with student actors or an inexperienced group, you can encourage this background work by suggesting the use of tools for exploration, such as the Character Analysis forms found in Appendices B and C. The Actor's Character Physical Analysis asks the actor to think deeply about the character's physical aspects, such as specific age, walk, stance, and vocal patterns. The Actor's Character

Background Analysis requires the actor to review the play for clues about the character's home life, religious and/or political influences, relationships, and other personal background factors as well as psychological indicators. Once completed, this content can be the basis for collaborative discussion throughout rehearsals. If you sense that your actors are experienced and are doing this work on their own, these forms may not be necessary. On the other hand, if you are working with younger, inexperienced actors or a community theatre group of newcomers, these forms may be quite helpful.

Additionally, you can use this initial meeting and read-through for orientation tasks. Many directors rely on this time to present their concept idea as well as the designers' visual presentations of the concept through set renderings and models, costume designs, and other design illustrations. When my directing projects have any historical or cultural context, I come to the initial rehearsal with photos I've gathered from my preparation research to aid my actors in grasping mood and atmosphere. I'll even play period music as the actors are entering the rehearsal hall for the same effect. Communication of your concept for the production is important early in the rehearsal process.

Each director approaches communication of concept uniquely. Noah Himmelstein's use of a single phrase to summarize the play's spine has served as a guiding beacon in his productions. He describes this process as follows:

> I identify what the play is about in a single phrase: what Harold Clurman would call the "spine." Despite much work on my own and with my team before rehearsals begin, I often go back to the single phrase – "for me, this play is about . . ." and solely that, whenever I get lost to get me back on track. With actors, all of this work is part of our discussions.

There are no right or wrong strategies. As a young director, you may want to experiment with methods of presenting your concept and see which ones most successfully lead to the path of discussion and questioning for your casts.

Early rehearsals are also an opportunity to begin to establish your collaborative working environment. As you observe your cast and the general interactions, can you think of exercises or activities to guide your cast to better collaboration? These activities may include group vocal and physical warmups before rehearsal begins, or inserting periodic trust exercises as you deem appropriate. Often something as simple as springing for a pizza after a long rehearsal can be a great bonding experience for your cast. In Chapters 2 and 3 we will explore specific activities and exercises to help you create and manage your positive working environment and encourage collaboration.

Conversely, the early rehearsals are a time for you to reflect on your own communication skills. Are you being clear with your messaging to both the creative team and actors? Are you using questions to provide an opportunity for feedback? Are you listening to responses with an open and honest ear? In Chapter 2 we will explore specific communication tools you can use in both production meetings and in the rehearsal room.

Blocking Rehearsals

These rehearsals are devoted to getting the play on its feet. As a novice director, I over-blocked and over-planned every single moment of each scene, fearful that I would look foolish in rehearsal if I didn't know what was going on at all times. This is a rooky mistake, and I caution you against doing the same! What I do suggest is that you have a clear understanding of general movement, entrances and exits, and any big moments such as chases, love scenes, or extraordinary stage business. Get through the basic blocking rehearsals quickly so that you can move into the refining rehearsals. If you have established the open, collaborative dialogue mentioned during the early rehearsals, then blocking rehearsals will be less tedious because both you and your actors will be creating together.

Refining Rehearsals

This is a time for you and your cast to collaborate on the movement, the relationships, and the connection to the concept of the play – where the real shaping happens. If you have created an open environment, questions may arise, brainstorming may occur, and growth may surge daily. Use your concept word/phrase/metaphor as a guide if rehearsals get derailed or bogged down. Break down the play into workable scenes or beats and as time progresses expand these into larger sections or run-throughs. The director is the liaison between the audience and the onstage creative process, so constantly check in as if you are an audience member viewing the production for the first time. Try closing your eyes and listening to a scene as an experiment. Watch a scene simply for movement patterns or balance or awkward stage business. Make sure you are moving around in the auditorium, checking sightlines and projection from all the seats in the house. Finally, watch the run-throughs with the eyes and ears of an audience member.

Tech Week

This is where all the technical aspects of the production begin to come together. Lights are added and tweaked. Sound and special effects are timed. Actors wear their costumes and changes are implemented. Set changes are layered in. Rehearsal props are replaced with real props.

The focus of the director shifts from actor to the design elements with a constant guiding question leading the way: Is the story clear for the audience? Actors may feel abandoned because the director must now focus on the design element's impact on the story. Leadership and communication skills are called into play to address constant last-minute decisions, emergencies, changes, and rising tensions. By dress rehearsal, the goal is that any technical snags have been ironed out and the entire production is running smoothly and professionally.

While tech week can be stressful, I have found that these tensions can be substantially reduced by laying the groundwork for a positive experience from the beginning of the production. How can you do this? In early collaborations with the creative team, ask about tech week requirements and any special needs, making sure that these needs are incorporated. In professional and academic venues, a paper tech (a sit-down meeting with director, stage manager, and light and sound crew to pencil in cues for the show prior to tech) is generally scheduled by the production coordinator and is well worth the time to iron out cues before bringing in the cast and crew.

Prior to tech week, consistently communicate the expectations to the cast at each refining rehearsal as tech draws near. Remind the actors that during tech week your responsibility as director changes. You will be watching their performances with a new focus: Is the playwright's story clear, or are the production elements inhibiting the telling of the story in any way? In projects where I have laid this groundwork, honored the rehearsal schedule throughout the process, encouraged the actors to stay on schedule, and communicated effectively to the entire ensemble, the tech rehearsals have been most productive.

Conclusion

You now have a better understanding of the director's challenge: to gain mastery of a range of directorial skills while incorporating the fundamental tasks required during the three phases of the directing project. Additionally, you have been introduced to the concepts of leadership and communication in directing, which we will explore in depth subsequently. Our goal is to understand why the collaborative theatre environment is so essential for the success of your directing project, and how to create not only that collaborative frame of mind, but also how to manage your positive working environment. These are the topics of Chapters 2 and 3.

Activities for Self-Reflection

Using your journal, respond to the following prompts relating to the concepts introduced in Chapter 1.

1 Famous director and theatre critic Harold Clurman has described the job of director as consisting of being "an organizer, a teacher, a politician, a psychic detective, a lay analyst, a technician, a creative being." Do you agree or disagree? In what ways do you see yourself as an organizer, a teacher, a politician, a psychic, an analyst, a technician, and a creative being when you direct?

2 Review the list of skills a director must possess and evaluate yourself in terms of your strengths in:

- Coordinating
- Delegating
- Guiding
- Advising
- Empowering
- Participating
- Managing

Jot down an example that demonstrates your use of three of these skills. Remember that no one expects you to be a master of every one of these skills, but reflecting and understanding your strengths early on will make you a better collaborator overall.

3 The chapter mentions the adjectives "courageous," "motivational," "disciplined," "respectful," "fair," "adaptable," "egoless," and "mindful" as characteristics of a strong leader. Are there other characteristics that you would add to the list? Which of these characteristics do you feel that you already possess? Which of these do you feel you need to work on?

4 Were you aware of the preparation phase of the directorial process? Do you read and analyze a play for aesthetic, historical, and cultural emphasis regularly? How deeply have you researched and explored the plays and playwrights of your past directing projects? Can you see how this process can add depth to future projects?

5 Do you have a set audition regime? What is it? Have you considered changing your auditions to fit with the type of production you are directing? What are some changes you might make in your normal audition routine in the future? Have you developed a guiding principle for casting your future plays?

6 What is your usual approach to the first day of rehearsal? Have you considered adapting your "first day" approach to fit with the type of production you are directing? What factors might dictate a change in approach?

Return to your journal and review your responses as you work through this guide. Feel free to add new insights and perspectives as you continue to evolve and grow as a person and a director.

Notes

1 Bloom, Michael. Introduction. *Thinking Like a Director: A Practical Handbook*. Faber and Faber, 2001, p. 4.
2 Clurman, Harold. *On Directing*. Macmillan, 1972, p. 14.
3 Hamilton's America: About the Documentary. *PBS Great Performances*, www.pbs.org/wnet/gperf/hamiltons-america-documentary/5048. Accessed February 6, 2019.
4 Ball, William. *A Sense of Direction: Some Observations on the Art of Directing*. Drama Publishers, 1984, p. 93.
5 Clurman, p. 28.
6 Ball, p. 35.
7 Sievers, W. David, Harry E. Stiver, Jr., and Stanley Kahan. *Directing for the Theatre*. Wm. C. Brown Co. Publishers, 1974, p. 49.
8 Bloom, pp. 69–80.
9 Dean, Alexander and Lawrence Carra. *Fundamentals of Play Directing*. Holt, Rinehart and Winston, 1974, p. 310.
10 Ball, p. 105.

Chapter 2

Creating a Positive Environment for Theatre Collaboration

Why is creating a positive environment for theatre collaboration so essential? The answer is both simple and monumental. Author Robert Knopf provides insights in his text *The Director as Collaborator*, when he offers:

> Encouraging everyone in the ensemble to create a part of the production rather than simply to execute the director's detailed ideas not only engenders goodwill, but it also gets each person's mind working toward the same end and frequently breaks down the traditional barriers and more than occasional rifts between production areas.[1]

Breaking down barriers, creating goodwill, and encouraging artistry are tasks best achieved in a positive theatre environment by a director who is both a strong leader and an open collaborator. The simple reasons why you will want to strive for this type of collaborative environment in your own practice are twofold: It makes you a better director, and it inspires creativity. Let's examine how this is true.

Have you ever been involved in a creative project, as a director, actor, or designer, where you constantly questioned yourself? Perhaps this was caused by the leadership, the overall environment, or merely your own insecurity. Regardless, you found it impossible to suppress that negative, self-doubting voice in your head. You know – that annoying voice that questions every move, each new idea, any out-of-the-box thinking you might want to attempt. In your role as director, when your creative team and actors stop working as a collaborative unit, you stop feeding off their energy and eventually your directorial juices dry up. You may easily give in to that nagging chatterbox.

On the other hand, when you establish a positive environment from the very beginning, there is less chance for those nagging voices of self-doubt to break through. When the ensemble feel respected and safe, they are more willing to take creative risks. When ideas are flowing and building upon one another abundantly between you, your creative team, and cast, you are free to tap into your imagination and so are they. And ultimately, when the ensemble experience ownership in the project, productivity will increase as well.

When I was a young actor, the summer before attending college, I was involved in a new play directed by the playwright. It was a difficult project because this young man really was not a director, but the play was "his baby" and he wanted full control of its destiny. The problem began immediately in the environment he established at rehearsals. I'm sure this playwright/director had a clear vision of the play in his head, but unfortunately he lacked the skills to communicate, guide, empower, or lead the cast. As actors, we were not inspired to create or take any risks with our characters, and he seemed quite impatient when actors asked questions, so we soon stopped doing so. The play did open, but it was very stiff and was drudgery to perform. In this case, the director could have taken steps to help establish the creative collaborative environment to lead to the success of the production. Looking back on that experience, I believe the playwright/director simply did not have the skills or awareness necessary.

Sometimes, however, the culture of the theatre organization is such that as hard as you try to create a collaborative environment, you are fighting a losing battle. For example, I once directed a summer stock production of a Theatre for Young Audience play, *Puss in Boots*, where I experienced no buy-in to my artistic concept from the creative staff. The set designer and the lighting designer were firmly ensconced in their own agendas. The attitude was: "Hey, this is how we do things around here, and you're an outsider." Sadly, I made the mistake of not standing up for myself and my vision. The lighting was a mish-mash of nonsensical cues with no cohesiveness and certainly no aesthetic connection to the concept I had tried to communicate. The palace set was very nice, but because the characters left the stage to travel through the audience quite a bit, I had requested some ideas to extend the set beyond the edges of the stage, perhaps adding some stylized trees or bushes. These ideas were immediately dismissed. I eventually gave up trying to work with the creative team, which in turn meant that we stopped stimulating each other for new ideas to improve the show. Unfortunately, the production suffered due to my lack of communication and my lack of strength of leadership.

On the other hand, I directed a professional production for Theatre on the Hill in Westminster, Maryland of a Theatre for Young Audiences play, *The Christmas Toys*, which resulted in a wonderful collaborative effort between both the production team and the actors. The set designer and scene painter as well as lighting, special effects, and costume designers each grasped my concept fully and worked beautifully together to coordinate their efforts. For example, the set designer provided several sketches to me, then altered the designs after realizing that some of the furniture needed to be practical while some remained within the painted scenery. The lighting designer, through production meeting discussions, came up with a fantastic idea of including lights inside a large trunk, so that whenever the trunk lid opened, bright lights magically glowed on the toy characters' faces. The production team scheduled periodic meetings to review progress and update necessary changes as rehearsals progressed. In addition, the rehearsals with the actors were free-flowing, creative, and fun. We used improvisation regularly to help actors develop the physical aspects of the toy characters in a shop. The entire production was built on a foundation of trust and respect for each other's knowledge, skills, and roles. What a delightful experience!

For actors working in an accepting, safe, collaborative environment, the possibilities are abundant. There is freedom to take risks, to let the imagination run free, and to create without fear. I directed a group-devised participation play, *The Tortoise and the Hare*, at Theatre on the Hill in Westminster, Maryland where I created the plot outline and the basic characters required. The actors fleshed out the characters in their own unique ways during the rehearsal process. For instance, the cat became a peppy cheerleader, interjecting choreographed cheers throughout the play, the dog became a grunge teen, and the referee skunk was a nervous wreck. Hilarious! These actors trusted each other, my guidance, and the environment we developed, and together we created a fun, well-received production of *The Tortoise and the Hare*.

As you are looking ahead to your next directing project or your first professional production, what will you need to focus on to create a positive theatre environment for your ensemble? What does a positive collaborative environment look like? The following are the characteristics that rise to the top for many of the directors I've interviewed and researched: safety, respect, positive attitude, free flow of ideas, and productivity.

Safety

Physical Safety

It goes without saying, anytime an actor is required to jump off, fall into, be covered up, hang from, be pushed into, wrestle with, be hit by (the list goes on, but I think you get the picture), safety is of the utmost importance. Falls must be choreographed. Rehearsal time must be set aside to test any sort of hanging or fly rigging for safety, and operators must be well trained (generally from a hired company that specializes in fly rigging, for example). Time for fight choreography or sword work must be well planned and rehearsed under the safest of conditions, with mats, appropriate equipment, and most importantly, with an experienced consultant, as mentioned earlier. Actors should never be bruised or cut up as a result of your stage direction, but it happens regularly because of poor planning or lack of concern by some directors.

In an extreme example, I directed a college production of Aurand Harris' *Punch and Judy* at Western Maryland College in Westminster, Maryland. The play is based on the British Punch and Judy puppet plays that are frankly rather dark and violent, featuring puppets that beat each other with bats, a scary devil, and a hanged man. Of course, we had many safety features in place to hang the student actor playing the hanged man. My greater concern centered on the devil character, who had the task of controlling a special effect – shooting a fireball from his hand upon his entrance. This is really not a complicated special effect, and we had a pyro expert teach him (several times) how to set off the device. We allowed plenty of rehearsal time, but this actor simply had a mental block about this moment in the play. First, he would forget to shoot the fireball or shoot it late. Next, he would shoot the fireball into the audience – a huge no-no! By tech week, we were getting worried, but the special effect was so impressive that we hated to cut it and the actor was sure he could master it. Putting our heads together, we created a target on the set, upstage (away from the audience!). By dress rehearsal, I felt confident that the actor was getting the hang of the device. However, during the third show in the run, our devil somehow missed the upstage target and shot the fireball across the stage and into the puppet stage at stage right. The puppet stage was draped with fabric, which slowly began to burn. I remember sitting in the last row of theatre with the set designer, saying, "Is the set on fire? I believe the set is on fire." Thank goodness some quick-thinking students backstage reached out and rolled the puppet stage offstage. The theatre was equipped with fire extinguishing materials, and at the next appropriate moment, the puppet stage was rolled back into place. The actors carried on as if nothing unusual had occurred, and many in the audience thought it was part of the play. A good lesson in safety is making sure that any space you use is equipped with fire extinguishers!

Your duty to keep your actors safe goes beyond fire protection, however. If your production requires sword play, street fights, even chase scenes, you have an obligation to protect your actors. Although I've taken courses in stage combat, I know that fight choreography is not my strength nor am I certified in this area. If I am directing a production that requires a realistic fist fight or sword play, it is my responsibility to maintain a safe environment for my actors, and I plan on hiring a stage combat expert to stage that scene. That's not a failing on my part; that's creating a safe environment and demonstrating leadership.

On the other hand, West Coast director Kate Danley describes the type of director who approaches rehearsals without any preparation and allows the actors complete latitude to figure out the blocking on their own. To some this may seem like great freedom; but to most veteran actors this is pure lack of leadership and rarely leads to the collaborative and safe environment we've been discussing. Kate gives a terrifying example of an unsafe situation she once experienced as an actor:

> I was in a show once where the director was acting too and he wanted to "figure things out." In that first blocking day, he decided with no warning that his character was going to throw a punch at my face. You know, for "emotional realism." I quit the next day.

When the actors and crew know that the director has their backs and takes this responsibility seriously, they begin to relax into the environment. Pulling in consultants who are experts in stage combat or special effects demonstrates respect for your ensemble.

Mental Safety

Safety doesn't stop with just the physical. Directors need to be tuned into psychological situations as well. In some productions, cliques develop. This can create a situation where certain actors feel like outcasts. Of course, some actors simply like to keep to themselves and that is a choice they have made. However, there are times when groupings begin to happen within a cast that start to exclude a few members. As the director, it's a good idea to watch for this and have a few tools to nip it in the bud early in rehearsals. I don't suggest making a big deal about what you may observe, but rather use the theatre tools at hand. I always felt it was worth the extra ten minutes out of my rehearsal time, especially if it strengthened the bond of my cast. In the next chapter I describe several warmup activities, trust games, and theatre games which can be helpful in building comradery and laying the groundwork for your collaborative framework.

Unfortunately, there are times when an actor may bring emotional baggage into the rehearsal hall, causing a disruption to the positive flow you've worked so hard to create. You are not expected to be a trained psychologist and know how to diagnose these situations. While there are times when a bit of compassion and skills in guiding and advising can come into play, you need to balance your genuine concern for one individual with your concern for the health of the ensemble. And you need to know your own limitations. Offering a kind expression of concern if an actor comes into rehearsal out of sorts and unable to work once is one thing. However, if the disruption continues or an actor shows signs of major distress, referring the actor to a professional for help is encouraged. In the academic setting, there are many resources available to you as a director. As you begin to find directing work with teens or young people in after school theatre programs or private schools, for example, be sure to ask about referral policies and procedures. For the mental safety of the actor and for others, the director will need to monitor the situation, keep the channels of communication open, and remain diligent.

Respect

The ultimate goal is giving and getting respect within your collaborative environment both in the production meetings and in the rehearsal studio. By respectfully listening to the ideas of your designers during production meetings, you are demonstrating a willingness to collaborate. As acting teacher and director Richard Pilcher offers: "Often the designers bring great new ideas to the table, and the director has to be prepared to go in a somewhat new direction as a result of the input . . . ." I also believe that a simple "thank you" goes a long way in demonstrating the respect I have for everyone on my production team, from designers to coordinators to crew members. I constantly reflect on the fact that every project I work on can only be successful when we all work together, and I also benefit by working with and learning from these artists.

Several "best practices" during rehearsals will demonstrate respect toward your actors. Being respectful of actors' time means not only having a plan for rehearsals, but also being disciplined enough to stick to the plan. For example, it is disrespectful to only work on Scene 1 when Scenes 1–4 are scheduled and you have actors sitting around who may only appear in Scene 4. In the rehearsal studio, adopting a philosophy of "safety first" and making sure it is communicated clearly demonstrates respect for your entire team. By taking the time to observe how each actor approaches character work and the craft of acting in the early days of rehearsal, you will be showing interest in the individuals. Being honest and fair may sound obvious, but can reap great results. Independent actor, director and author Kate Danley offers: "Speak the truth if someone is slacking. Speak the truth if something isn't working. When you speak the truth, no matter how hard or uncomfortable, it allows your team to trust that you won't allow them to look bad." Sometimes being honest and fair means carrying the full load of responsibility on your shoulders, but the mutual respect you receive from your ensemble is well worth it.

Finally, you show respect in the way you speak and listen to your cast and production team throughout the production process. As a role model, you demonstrate respect through your leadership decisions and guidance. In Chapter 3, several important communication tools as well as leadership skills are introduced, along with activities that invite collaboration.

Positive Attitude

As director and leader, you need to demonstrate a positive attitude at every creative meeting, from your first encounter with your potential actors at auditions to the pre-production designer meetings to every rehearsal. In the examples above, it is easy to see how a disciplined, prepared approach can create a respectful space, which translates into a positive working environment. As directors, in what other ways can our positive attitude help to create a collaborative working environment? Hamilton Clancy, Artistic Director for The Drilling Company in New York City, believes: "If you're directing a play, you need to be ready to inspire everyone to climb the mountain, no matter how uncertain. You need to be unflappable." Positive, unflappable leadership can be inspirational, and provide the solid foundation for both your actors and creative team to take risks, experiment, and be at ease.

Does positive attitude mean only providing positive approval and agreeing with everything our creative team and actors throw at us? Do we simply praise our actors' every move and encourage our creative teams' every effort? This is the challenge and the confusion. Positive attitude does not necessarily mean always saying "yes," "good," "great." Knowing when to experiment during rehearsal and when to rein in your actors using your well-defined concept as your guide is part of the balancing act. Listening to your creative team's ideas but knowing when to say "no" to an idea that contradicts your concept shows leadership. Being disciplined, prepared, and open to feedback – these are good starts.

Positive attitude begins even prior to the rehearsals. How do you present yourself during the audition process? Have you thought about how you'd like to greet each actor or group of actors upon arrival? These initial moments of contact are your opportunity to begin creating the positive environment which can go a long way in setting the stage for opening communication and generating collaboration with your actors.

Consider the following two audition scenarios.

Early in my career I auditioned for a production of *Company* at a reputable community theatre in the Chicago area. The audition consisted of a group dance routine and then individually singing sixteen bars of a show tune before scene readings. The choreographer ran the dance portion, and the stage manager ran the vocal auditions and organized the paired readings, while a panel of four important-looking theatre professionals sat in the audience – presumably the director, assistant director and perhaps the producers. This group never introduced themselves nor interacted with the auditionees throughout the entire audition process. I did receive a small role in the show and finally met the director, of course. But the truth about this show was that the entire experience and environment were very cold. The cast never bonded, and I believe it was because of the lack of directorial leadership and communication, beginning at my very first encounter – the audition.

On the other hand, I once auditioned for a professional production of *A Christmas Carol* for Totem Pole Playhouse in Chambersburg, Pennsylvania. Based on most of my auditioning experiences for professional companies, I expected to be called into the theatre (or a rehearsal room), make the long walk to the stage, where I would stand in front of the director and production assistant, whose faces would be hidden behind resumes. After presenting my prepared monologue, I'd leave. But something amazing happened at this particular audition, and I've never forgotten it. As I made the long walk down the theatre aisle to the stage, Totem Pole Artistic Director Carl Schurr greeted me at the foot of the stage, hand extended, introduced himself, and chatted a bit. He immediately put me at ease. What a novel idea! What a compassionate idea! This is someone with whom I would love to work and collaborate, I thought to myself.

Ever since that audition encounter with Carl Schurr, I've kept that moment in mind when I run my own auditions. How can I make my actors feel more comfortable? How can I communicate that working with me will be a collaborative process, that I will be a friendly, compassionate director? I can start with a simple greeting and a hand shake, if practical; I can engage each actor in conversation; I can work with the actor by requesting an adjustment to the reading; I can thank the actor for auditioning.

Free Flow of Ideas

A free flow of ideas and innovation is yet another characteristic of a positive theatre environment. By establishing a safe space for your actors and creative team to create, take risks, even fail and try a new approach, you are encouraging ideas to germinate and develop. This free flow of ideas can occur throughout the collaborative process – during auditions, in rehearsal, and in production meetings.

As a direct result of Mr. Schurr's inspiring encounter, my audition routine as director for *The Christmas Toys* was greatly impacted. As previously mentioned, this play for young audiences required the majority of the adult actors to play toys in a toyshop. I knew that prepared monologues or script readings would not tell me much about the actors at the initial audition. I also knew that I needed to make my auditionees feel as relaxed as possible in order for me to observe physical, toy-like characterizations. Instead of the traditional script reading, I met the actors on stage and lead a few quick warmups and theatre games with the goal of creating a relaxed environment where the auditionees would feel comfortable to create freely. Next I facilitated several toy-related character improvisations, rotating different pairs of actors to be as fair as possible. For example, I was looking for a soldier, puppet doll, and floppy clown character. I also asked the actors to experiment with character voices that might match these body movements. Beyond improvisation skills, I was looking for physical agility, creative vocal work, risk-taking, and group cooperation. By warming up the group and helping them relax, the auditionees responded with an array of free flowing, creative ideas – from stiff-legged walking and precision marching soldiers to jerky and floppy puppet moves to freely swaying and clumsy clown gestures – all providing me with excellent audition data from which to make my casting selections.

When a director enters rehearsals with the entire show completely blocked down to the last detail, every angle of subtext pre-discovered, and every question answered, the actors will feel stifled. There is no journey for the cast to take. By demonstrating your willingness to explore together and collaborate, while asking questions and listening to the actors' ideas, you lay the groundwork for more risk-taking and flow of ideas in the rehearsal studio. Acting teacher and independent director Richard Pilcher reminds us: "Try an idea if it seems good to you, and if it doesn't work out, drop it and move on. Rehearsal is about experimenting." This process may result in new ideas, modified ideas, or unused ideas. Actors are stimulated – creativity and ideas flowing.

Likewise, with the creative team it is important to demonstrate your willingness to explore and collaborate together when you are introducing your concept ideas during the early production meetings. In fact, many designers desire this type of collaborative environment, seeking feedback, questions, and even guidance from the director. Professional New York and regional theatre set designer Jo Winiarski states: "I'm always disappointed when I walk in with my model and the director simply says 'That's great.' I can only generate so much myself. A tough director makes me a better designer."[2]

Striking a balance between discussing in a give-and-take manner and "dictating" your vision for the design elements is your constant goal. Listen first, ask questions next, and listen some more. In my experience, designers are creative experts whose talents simply need to be tapped for this particular project. Once tapped, the ideas flow freely. Award-winning lighting designer Jaymi Smith has said of working with collaborative directors: "I like directors who want me to be part of the conversation, who want me to help develop the story with them, but who will push me and extend my vision."[3] By encouraging the conversation, you are generating the creative energy to spur a flow of ideas.

Encouragement of discussion with your creative team doesn't always have to be elaborate. For example, after listening to the set designer's initial's thoughts, a very simple "What if . . .?" question can open up a number of possibilities, allowing creative options to flow freely. This occurred during a production meeting for a Theatre for Young Audiences production I directed of *Androcles and the Lion* at Carroll Community College in Westminster, Maryland. The set was a large backyard playset borrowed from a retail vendor. It included two separate units connected by a monkey bar ladder, two slides, climbing ropes, and side ladders. When the playset arrived, unbeknownst to anyone on the design team, it also included a huge plastic tube, about six feet long and three feet wide. The set designer and I collaborated using "What if . . .?" to generate a flow of ideas to utilize this tube within the set. Although I had already blocked, rehearsed, and refined most of the play in the rehearsal studio, I had prepped the cast that there would be changes once we moved onto the stage and began working on the actual playset. In addition to some of the ideas generated during the production meeting for incorporating the tube, I encouraged the actors to come up with moments within the play when the tube could be used. The actors found ways to hide inside, jump over, sit on, reach over, and hide behind the tube. Collaborating together, the set designer, the actors, the technical director, and I also developed five set changes that incorporated movement of the tube. The actors had a sense of ownership in the process, emanating from their own free flow of ideas.

Productivity

When you have created a collaborative setting, the process is satisfying and just plain fun. Everyone feels productive, takes ownership of the project, and works hard for success. On the other hand, you've probably experienced a production in the past when you just couldn't wait for rehearsals be over. I know I have. Maybe it was due to overall disorganization, the director's controlling nature, or maybe it was because of several toxic cast members. Several ways a director can squash the productivity of the ensemble include: (1) over-rehearsing the play or not managing the rehearsal time well, (2) dictating to the actors (or designers), (3) not demonstrating a positive attitude or blaming others rather than taking responsibility when things go awry, and (4) not including the actors' (or designers') input.

In the best scenarios, however, when you are striving to respect your creative team and cast by doing your play analysis and being prepared for production meetings, being disciplined in rehearsals and honoring your actors' time, working collaboratively with your actors and creative team so that ideas flow freely, considering your actors' safety, and demonstrating a positive attitude, productivity will result. In the collaborative theatre environment you have created, your cast and creative team will respond because they feel respected. They feel inspired to create and contribute. They feel ownership in the project. They want the project to succeed and to be a part of that success.

The following are three practices you can incorporate into your rehearsals to assist in developing productivity. Once you have established a collaborative working environment, these practices will intensify the feeling of ownership and pride the actors will feel in the project, and their response will follow. These practices include: *managing rehearsal mayhem*, *goal-setting* at the beginning of each rehearsal and a *closing activity* for each rehearsal.

As a director, you hope your actors will stay in character and concentrate throughout the rehearsal process, particularly during run-throughs. However, some breaking and fun during early rehearsals can result in creative discoveries. The trick is to strive for balance. When you have mutual respect with your cast, it is easier to set limits and not lose control of your rehearsals altogether. Be careful that bad habits aren't forming in the early rehearsals. One method is to *manage rehearsal mayhem*. You can try to get a scene back on track with a gentle, "Oops, okay. Since we've stopped, let's think about (ask a subtext question, for example)." Then ask the stage manager to get the actors back on track with an appropriate starting line. Or you might consider taking a short break and regrouping altogether. Regardless, in the rehearsal studio, where you've created a positive working environment, your ensemble will be more likely to respond to your gentle prompts than to a director who resorts to yelling or threats. That is a sure way to lose the respect and positive attitude you have worked so hard to build.

Another powerful practice is *goal-setting* at the beginning of each rehearsal. This can be a simple statement such as "The purpose of today's rehearsal is . . ." or can involve the actors' input such as "In addition to the scheduled scene work, are there any moments we have overlooked that need attention?" In the broader sense, this simple activity allows the actors to feel they are a larger part of the process.

Finally, ending each rehearsal with a question, either relating back to your goal-setting at the beginning of rehearsal or broadening, can be an excellent *closing activity* as well as a bonding moment for the cast. Asking "What did we achieve/learn/grasp this evening?" should not be consider an academic exercise, only to be used in the college or high school setting. You can adapt the activity for the community theatre, New Play Festival, or small professional theatre directing project as well. As with the goal-setting practice, when actors feel a sense of ownership of the process, they also feel a sense of responsibility to the success of the project. This translates to productive work habits, like getting off book on time, getting to rehearsal on time and ready to work, and a willingness to concentrate and stay in character (or get back into character after a break), for example.

Whether your next directing project takes place in the college theatre lab, a Theatre for Young Audience venue, or a community theatre, I encourage you to keep these five characteristics of a positive environment for theatre collaboration in mind: safety, respect, positive attitude, free flow of ideas, and productivity. As award-winning theatre director and author Michael Bloom reminds us:

> Ultimately the director is a "creator of communities" – someone who can recognize talent and inspire the very best from other artists, lead them but welcome their contributions, and make everyone feel they are important partners.[4]

Conclusion

Suppressing the negative voice of self-doubt is essential in order for directors to tap into personal creative impulses as well as those of their creative teams and actors. By creating a positive collaborative theatre environment for your next directing project, you will not only stretch as a director, but also inspire creativity in your ensemble. Creating a foundation of safety, respect, positivity, a free flow of ideas, and productivity for both your creative team and actors will set the stage for collaborative exchange. In Chapter 3 you will discover specific communication techniques and theatre activities as well as leadership skills to help you manage your own collaborative theatre environment.

Activities for Self-Reflection

Using your journal, respond to the following prompts relating to the concepts introduced in the preceding chapter.

1   Are there times when you've been aware of a "nagging chatterbox" filling your head with self-doubt about a creative decision or project? Reflect on one or two of those situations and consider the following:

   a   Were there any outside factors that may have influenced this negative voice, including the environment, the people, or the material/content?
   b   Was this negative voice fueled by internal factors, including memories of past experiences and personal insecurities?
   c   How did you respond to that inner voice? What actions did you take?

2   Ask yourself the following questions about your personal auditioning strategies:

   a   What message do you want to communicate to potential cast members for your current production and for future projects?

    b   Decide how you can incorporate that message into your general audition process. Break your process into steps. What do you think each step communicates?

    c   Share your process with your class or other theatre colleagues and listen to feedback.

3   Have you ever been involved in a production or scene project where you felt disrespected or unsafe? If so, how did that feeling affect your creativity or your overall attitude about the project?

4   What would you like your rehearsal/production environment to look like in terms of the following:

    a   Safety
    b   Respect
    c   Positive attitude
    d   Free flow of ideas
    e   Productivity

5   Do you consider yourself a "creator of communities" as Michael Bloom suggests in this chapter? In what ways to do you see yourself and your directing projects creating communities?

Don't be afraid to return to your journal and review your responses as you work through this guide. Feel free to add new insights and perspectives as you continue to evolve and grow as a person and a director.

Notes

1 Knopf, Robert. Introduction. *The Director as Collaborator*. Routledge, 2016, p. 2.
2 Cohen, Robert. *Working Together in Theatre: Collaboration and Leadership*. Palgrave Macmillan, 2011, p. 96.
3 Cohen, *Working Together in Theatre*, p. 96.
4 Bloom, Michael. Introduction. *Thinking Like a Director: A Practical Handbook*. Farrar, Straus and Giroux, 2001, p. 5.

Chapter 3

Managing the Collaborative Theatre Environment

You now have a conceptual understanding of how to create a collaborative working environment as an important foundation for your next directorial project. You are probably wondering: How do I manage this environment once I've created it? This chapter dives into the three components you will need to understand and eventually master with experience: (1) group dynamics in rehearsals, (2) three important communication tools to utilize in both the rehearsal hall and the designer meeting room, and (3) leadership skills in your overall directorial process. These are the building blocks for managing your collaborative theatre environment.

Group Dynamics

While a review of group dynamics – a system of behaviors within or between social groups – may not sound appropriate in a directing text, I can assure you it is beneficial to directing. Let's first examine the basic elements of group dynamics and then relate the model to the rehearsal hall. The origins of group dynamics can be traced as far back as 1896 and the beginnings of group psychology. While generally associated with psychology and sociology studies, group dynamics is finding application in business, education, sports, and even theatre practices. Within the broad field of group dynamics, there are many individual theories and theorists. As a model to use in the directorial process, psychologist and professor of education at the Walter E. Dennis Learning Center at Ohio State University Bruce Tuckman's four-stage model of group dynamics, known as Tuckman's Stages, is an excellent resource.[1]

Tuckman's classic group dynamics four-stage model includes:

- Forming – Group members initially get along, as they sort out what their role will be and how they fit into the group.
- Storming – Group members begin to abandon feigned politeness and friction begins, sometimes to the point of tempers flaring.

- Norming – Group members begin to get used to each other, developing trust and productivity.
- Performing – Group members are working together toward the common goal.

Any group will go through all four stages, and in fact it is a healthy process. As a director, having this knowledge will help you assist and lead your cast through all four stages. I will first describe each stage – Forming, Storming, Norming, and Performing – in terms of possible rehearsal interactions and behaviors. Following the group dynamics descriptions, I will offer warmups and exercises for each stage. By learning to read your actors, you can then incorporate a series of warmups and exercises into your rehearsals, helping to keep your cast from getting stuck in one stage and to move swiftly to the next. Your overarching goal is to build a safe and trusting environment for your ensemble so that collaboration flows freely.

In theatre, the group dynamics process occurs regularly. A unique cast are thrown together for the first read-through on day one of rehearsal. Perhaps a few cast members have worked together; perhaps a few cast members are brand new. There may be excitement and eagerness; there may be apprehension and even confusion. Some of the actors are outgoing, confident; others are a bit introverted. Welcome to the *Forming Stage*, where your cast will be spending precious energy sorting out exactly how they fit into this production.

Inevitably, you will have some sort of rehearsal drama – the *Storming Stage*. Cast members begin jockeying for power positions. Insecurities can cause egos to flare. Bickering, hard feelings, tempers, and bad attitudes can rear their ugly heads during the Storming Stage and waste valuable rehearsal time.

Once you are able to ease through the tension of the Storming Stage, your cast and staff can finally begin to focus on the project at hand. You have entered the *Norming Stage*. At this point, actors and creative staff begin to feel secure in their roles and are learning routines. Feeling safe in their work environment, they trust each other and you, and focus on the rehearsal process. These are the goals of the Norming Stage.

The *Performing Stage*, when the cast and staff finally work as a whole toward the success of the project, is every director's dream. Your cast are performing at peak energy, tuned into their highest levels of imagination and creativity, and are fully supporting each other. Sometimes a production never gets to this stage and the rehearsal process is pure drudgery. True, the director and cast may put together a decent show, but sadly, the group never realizes its full creative potential.

The goal, then, is to move as efficiently as possible through the Forming and Storming Stages, to get to the more comfortable and creative Norming and Performing Stages. How can you, as director, gently guide and lead your actors through these stages? Is it possible? The following exercises are a good place to begin.

Games and Activities for the Forming Stage – Ice Breakers, Theatre Games

Introductory Activities

The first day of rehearsal is your opportunity to establish the tone for the entire production period. Of course you want to let your cast know that you take this project seriously, but what else? What would you like the cast to take away from the first rehearsal that would be a great first step in building that safe and trusting environment? A sense of togetherness, a spirit of the mission, a family atmosphere? This goal may change depending on your project or concept. Be clear about this take-away before you meet your cast on day one.

You can incorporate a number of ice breaker activities in your first rehearsal. Depending on the size of your cast, your ice breaker activity could take the form of a focus game or be as simple as "Tell us your name and something unique about yourself." What you choose for an ice breaker may also reflect the type of production you are directing. For instance, *Oklahoma* or *Annie* with large casts and upbeat music take on a different "first day" feel than a more intimate drama. One ice breaker theatre game that I've used for large casts with great success is called Back to Back, a variation of Augusto Boal's Person to Person, Quebec-Style.[2]

Back to Back Game

Variation #1: Everyone finds a partner and stands back to back. The director/leader calls out two body parts and partners must touch these together (for instance, "Head to Head" or "Elbow to Knee"). After three sets of instructions, the director/leader calls out "Back to Back" and everyone scurries to find a new partner, standing back to back to begin another series.

Variation #2: This is the same as above, except that the instructions are cumulative, so that when the pair has put the first set of body parts together, the connection must stay intact while carrying out the next set of instructions. (In the example above, the pair must keep their heads together while figuring out how to secure an elbow to a knee.)

Warmup Activities

Professional actors are trained to warm up on their own and will budget time before each rehearsal for appropriate personal warmups. Student or amateur actors, however, can benefit from group warmups, and as a director trying to build a collaborative environment, so can you. Carving out time in your rehearsal schedule for group warmups, especially early in the process, can help you to observe your actors and learn about their tendencies, work habits, and attitudes. This is a great time to utilize basic physical and vocal warmups, but also weave in a few ice breakers and fun (but purposeful) theatre games during the Forming Stage of your cast's development.

The following are two simple routines you may want to consider in leading group warmups in your own rehearsals. You may have additional exercises to add or replace. Make the routines your own, or change them up to keep rehearsals fresh.

Physical Warmup Routine

Have your actors stand in a circle in a neutral position (feet hip distance apart, weight equally distributed, arms hanging freely, shoulders back and relaxed, chin level to the ground). Begin with the head and work down the body:

1   Head rolls – Drop chin to chest and slowly roll the head to the right until ear meets the right shoulder. Stop. Slowly roll chin toward chest and continue until ear meets the left shoulder. Stop. Repeat four times slowly. (Note: Avoid rolling neck in a full circle as this could cause harm to the vertebrae.)

2   Ear to shoulder stretches – From a neutral position, tilt left ear to left shoulder, feeling the stretch in right side of the neck. To add to the stretch, slowly raise the left arm and place the left hand on the side of right side of the face. Don't pull on the head, rather allow the weight of the hand to add to the stretch. For an even deeper stretch, pull away with the right arm. Hold for twenty or thirty seconds for a fuller stretch, then repeat on the other side. (Note: If any segment of this stretch is painful or too intense, back off or release a bit. There is nothing to be gained from pain.)

3   Shoulder scrunches and rolls – From a neutral position, raise the shoulders up to the ears and hold as tightly as possible. Hold for several seconds. Release with the sound of "Hah," also releasing any excess breath. Repeat three times. Next, slowly roll the shoulders forward, up to the ears, backward, and down in a large circle. Repeat the circle three times. Next, reverse the circle and repeat three times.

4   Rib isolations – From a neutral position, place hands on the bottom of the rib cage. Keeping the entire body aligned, move only the ribs to the right, then forward, to the left, then back, creating a slow circle. Feel a stretch in the mid and lower back. Repeat the circle four times in each direction.

5   Hip rolls – From a neutral position, place hand on the hips and bend the knees slightly. Keeping the entire body aligned, move only the hips to the right, then forward, to left, then back, creating a slow circle. Feel the stretch in the thighs and lower back. Repeat the circle four times in each direction.

6   Ankle twirlies – From a neutral position, while maintaining balance on the left foot, twirl right foot in large circle in one direction four times, then switch directions. Repeat with left foot, maintaining balance on the right foot.

Vocal Warmup Routine

Facial muscles – to stretch tight muscles in the face and jaw:

1   The Lion – On count of three, stick tongue out as far as possible with an "Ah" sound. Repeat three times.

2   Smush Face/Open Face – Squeeze the face muscles together as tightly as possible and hold. Next, open face muscles as wide as possible, stretching the eyes and mouth open. Repeat three times.

3   Yawning Jaw – Drop the jaw open as if yawning. Massage the face and jaw muscle, if tight.

Open sounds – to gently warm up vocal chords:

1   Humming – Take a deep breath from the diaphragm and hum on a single note, keeping lips closed. Whenever air is depleted, take another breath and begin humming again. (Note: Encourage the group to keep the humming strong, breathing when necessary and then rejoining the group, and to get in touch with the vibration of their vocal chords by placing a hand on the neck.)

2   Roller Coaster – Take a deep breath from the diaphragm and begin to hum on any note. Begin to slide slowly up the vocal scale as high as possible and then slide down as low as possible. Take a breath as air is depleted and rejoin the humming. (Note: It is helpful to lead the group with an arm gesture up and down, like a musical director conducting a choir.)

Isolating sounds – to loosen up the tongue, lips and jaw:

1   Emphasis on the consonant

       Lah – Lay – Lee – Lie – Loo – Loo
       Mah – May – Mee – Mie – Moh – Moo
       Pah – Pay – Pee – Pie – Poh – Poo

Kah – Kay – Kee – Kie – Koh – Koo
Nah – Nay – Nee – Nie – Noh – Noo

2   Consonant placement (notice the physical placement of these consonants and encourage clear distinction between each)

PPPPah (repeat with the consonants B, T, D, K, and G)

Articulation exercises:

1   Paper Poppy – Repeat four times
2   Baby Bubble – Repeat four times
3   Topeka – Repeat eight times
4   Mommala Poppala – Repeat four times
5   Fiddle dee dee/Fiddle dee dah – Repeat four times

Tongue twisters are fun, and there are many resources for these. However, I use tongue twisters sparingly and focus on articulation rather than speed. What I've observed is that misuse of tongue twisters only rein-forces bad habits, such as talking too fast and sloppy speech. (For more extensive vocal work and exercise regimes, see Kristen Linklater's *Freeing the Natural Voice*, listed in Appendix E.)

Games and Activities for the Storming Stage

As your cast move from the Forming to Storming Stage, you will want to help them ease through the transition as quickly as possible. Particularly if you are observing any divisiveness, sprinkling the occasional trust game into the group warmup, after a break or even during scene work, is a focused way to build group dynamics and lead your cast toward the ulti-mate prize: a positive, trusting, creative environment.

One of my favorite trust games for bringing together a group of diverse individuals is the Human Knot. I've used this in many situations: classes or workshops I've taught, casts I've directed, even an orchestra I was workshopping with the goal of group bonding! The effect is amazing, in that the activity forces the mini-groups to work together (collaborate) to complete the task. This isn't a new activity, although I am including a variation that isn't often introduced.

Human Knot (Basic)

Divide your cast or group into small circles of eight to twelve members. Ask them to stand in the circle, facing in, and cross their arms in front of them at the elbows. Next, they should step forward and grab some-one's hand, but they cannot grab the hand of the person next to them.

(This is very important – repeat this instruction!) Once everyone is connected, they are to disentangle, but remind them they cannot ever let go of the hand they are holding until the knot is untangled. Encourage talking among the group members to disentangle the knot. There are two possible results of this exercise: the knot will be untangled to create one large circle, or sometimes there will be two smaller circles. Encourage your group(s) that this challenge is solvable.

Human Knot (Variation)

The group circle(s) begin exactly the same as above, but once everyone is connected, they are not permitted to speak as they begin to disentangle. This forces the participants to rely on other means of communication to problem-solve: facial expression and body language.

In addition to the Human Knot, you may want to explore some paired trust exercises, but in the spirit of easing through the Storming Stage and working toward group bonding, just make sure you keep rotating the pairs. One I particularly like comes from Augusto Boal's *Games for Actors and Non-Actors* and is called the Leaning-against-each-other Trust Walk.[3]

Leaning-against-each-other Trust Walk (Paired)

Two actors stand side by side with their shoulders touching, and lean into each other. Each tries to keep his or her feet as far from the other person's feet as possible as the pair walks across the stage or room. A variation of this is to add another pair to the original pair, one person on either side.

The following are two additional trust exercises involving the entire ensemble working together and encouraging group bonding.

Count to Twenty

Actors stand in a tight circle, shoulder to shoulder. One actor begins by saying "One" out loud. At any point, a second actor says "Two," and the activity continues until the group reaches twenty. However, if at any time two actors start to say a number at the same time, the group must start again at "One." This activity requires concentration, eye contact, and trust. Once the group reach the goal of counting to twenty, they feel a great sense of accomplishment and cohesiveness, making it an ideal exercise to use during the Storming Stage.

Trust Circle

The Trust Circle works well if the play has strong themes or issues. Have cast members (and creative team/crew, if appropriate) sit in a circle and discuss how the theme of the play relates to own their own lives.

For example, during rehearsals for *The Miracle Worker*, a play about Annie Sullivan's work with Helen Keller, a trust circle discussion could focus on the themes of institutionalization versus education for special needs children. A leading question such as "Has anyone been touched by this issue in terms of a family member or friend?" can get the ball rolling. No one is required to participate, but even by simply listening, participants can discover renewed respect and understanding of their fellow ensemble members. This activity can be an effective tool in moving a group from the Storming to Norming Stage.

Continuing warmup activities, adding trust exercises, and encouraging discussions to foster group bonding are helpful in easing an ensemble through the Storming Stage. However, remember that this stage is a normal part of the group dynamic process. Your awareness and response can hasten the effects, and help to move the group to the more productive Norming Stage.

Activities for the Norming Stage – Improvising within the Script

You have helped your cast glide through Forming and Storming, and have arrived at a sense of normalcy in the rehearsal process. At this point, you may not need much in the way of activities to build up your group. However, your goal is to make sure your cast are 100% comfortable with the collaborative environment. As stated earlier, you want to create a rehearsal process that encourages input, inspires creativity, and supports a collaborative, artistic vision. A great activity at the Norming Stage in the group dynamics process is improvisation as a rehearsal tool.

An example of using improvisation during the Norming Stage occurred during my production of *Androcles and the Lion* at Carroll Community College in Westminster, Maryland. The set for this production was an outdoor playground. A stage direction in the script has the cast of six travelling Commedia dell'arte actors come upon the perfect site (in this case, the playground) to perform their show. Most of our rehearsals took place in a rehearsal studio until the final two weeks when the actors were able to work on the actual playground equipment – jungle gyms, ladders, slides, huge plastic tubes, ropes, you name it. I allowed for large portions of our rehearsal time, including warmups, to be devoted to exploring the space in a child-like manner. For example, the actors played tag, hide-and-seek, kick the can, and other childhood games on the set. In fact, we even began to incorporate some of the chase patterns and hiding places into the blocking. This became a collaborative, fun venture. Had I tried to over-block the chase scenes in the studio and force them to work once we moved onto the set, everyone would have been frustrated. Flexibility and the use of improvisation can be very beneficial during the Norming Stage.

Other uses for improvisation in the Norming Stage can occur during the refining rehearsals, especially as the cast are continuing to explore characterization and character relationships. For instance, improvising a scene for fluidity and emotional connection when the actors aren't off book yet can be very helpful. Improvisations of the imaginary scene prior to the text scene you are working on can help develop character background and character relationship. If a character entrance seems unbelievable or unmotivated, a short improvisation of the moment before the entrance can be extremely helpful to make the entrance more authentic. Finally, consider spending some rehearsal time improvising moments described by the playwright in the play that take place offstage. For example, in *The Glass Menagerie* actors could improvise a scene around Amanda's description of her visit to the business college she presumes her daughter Laura is attending. During the Norming Stage, when the cast are comfortable working as a group, improvisations can be a productive rehearsal tool.

Performing Stage

Once your cast and production team have worked through all the aspects of Forming, Storming, and Norming, they enter the desired stage of Performing. At this stage, there is little need of extra activities or exercises because your focus will be on maintaining good communication and creative collaboration. However, it is important to know that once a group achieves the Performing Stage, it may slip back to the Forming Stage at any time and you may need to briefly work through the stages again. For example, a change in circumstances, like a cast member replacement, can upset the balance and start the process over again. You will know the characteristics to look for and some exercises to help your cast move quickly from stage to stage.

Incorporating Three Important Communication Tools in Managing the Collaborative Theatre Environment

Let's focus on three effective communication tools you can use as you work collaboratively with your actors and creative team. These include the director's encouragement of brainstorming, active listening, and questioning.

Brainstorming

Madison Avenue advertising executive Alex Osborn developed the original brainstorming approach his 1953 book, *Applied Imagination: Principles and Procedures of Creative Problem-Solving.*[4] Often used in business and educational environments to problem-solve and come up with creative solutions, brainstorming is useful in the theatrical world as well to help actors and designers fully participate in a nonjudgmental atmosphere.

One method of brainstorming is individual brainstorming. Team members find a quiet time and place to contemplate the issue at hand, jotting down possible solutions or ideas, without self-criticizing or analyzing, for a designated period of time. Upon completion, the team member can review and evaluate the list for potential solutions. Group brainstorming follows a similar procedure, although the group assign a recorder to document each member's contributions. Again, it is critical that the participants should simply allow ideas to flow without any initial discussion or analysis, as tempting as it may be. At the end of the allotted time, the group can then discuss and analyze the practicality of the solutions presented.[5]

I directed *A Thousand Cranes* at Carroll Community College in Westminster, Maryland to open the campus' new performing arts center. The new theatre had minimal tools for set building, no stock set pieces, props or costumes, and limited lighting instruments. Through group brainstorming, the production team were able to create a list of costume and lighting resources within the community where we could borrow items needed for the show. Additionally, these group brainstorming sessions led to other "What if . . .?" questions, such as "What if we invited elementary school students to see the show?" This inquiry then manifested into a county grant for bussing elementary students to six matinee performances to full houses, complete with a full-color study guide funded by the college.

Encourage your actors and creative team to participate in individual and group brainstorming and introduce the idea of "What if . . .?" to open their minds and imagination. Additionally, think of the possibilities of this process in connecting your production to the community at large: connecting with a community action group that aligns with your play's theme and inviting a representative to post-show talkbacks; taking part in a community arts festival; creating a pre-show art or cultural exhibit in the lobby curated by a local art center or historical society; and the list goes on.

As you add additional communication skills to the use of brainstorming, such as active listening and questioning, you will be setting the stage for collaborative work. These types of communication skills demonstrate respect for your actors and creative team and inspire a creative response. Let's continue by exploring how active listening and questioning can be used to motivate collaboration.

Active Listening

One of the best ways to demonstrate respect for another person is listening. In fact, every current professional director I canvassed for feedback for this book mentioned listening as a crucial directorial skill. Dallas Munger of The Chalkboard Players cautions:

> The biggest communication pitfall that I have seen directors fall into is not listening enough . . . . Take time to consider others' opinions even if you don't end up following their advice. Don't fall into the trap of being defensive about your ideas as a director. Ultimately, you have the power to decide, so hearing out someone's idea and considering it or even giving it a try before making the decision to go a different direction can't hurt your creative process. Often, I find that the whole idea may not work, but in the process of trying something new, a positive discovery about the scene or a character is made . . . .

Munger's advice applies during production meetings with your creative team and throughout the rehearsal process with your acting ensemble. In fact, as a director, your excellent listening skills may help ease the transition of your cast through the group dynamics stages more efficiently, because you will be more tuned in to the characteristics of Forming, Storming, and Norming, as described earlier.

What is meant by active listening? This is a communication skill that requires the listener to be fully present for the speaker – fully concentrating, understanding, responding, and processing the message. As a director, mastery of this tool is essential in demonstrating respect for and building trust with your actors and creative team. Active listening can be comprised of the following techniques: *concentrating on the speaker, being aware of body language, being open and non-judgmental,* and *demonstrating understanding.*

Concentrating on the speaker: In the rehearsal hall or the production meeting, your ensemble deserve your undivided attention. Concentration involves giving your full attention with your mind and heart, and tuning in mentally to what the speaker is saying. Needless to say, this means setting aside other activities, like writing notes, looking at your watch, texting or reading emails. Give your full attention to the actor's or designer's message, rather than formulating your response or rebuttal.

Being aware of body language: Be aware that active listening is more than simply processing the words being spoken by another person: it involves physically listening as well. Sit or stand up straight and look at the speaker's eyes. Keeping your body open and leaning in toward the speaker will show your interest and willingness to engage, rather than sitting back with your arms crossed. Nodding your head encourages expansion of the ideas expressed. Equally, by taking in the body positions, facial and vocal expressions of the speaker, you will get a true sense of their message. Body language awareness is a two-way street in both the rehearsal hall and during production meetings.

Being open and non-judgmental: As you are listening to the actor's input or the creative team member's ideas, be fully open to the potential and try not to pre-judge. Listen to the complete version of each point or concept. Allow the idea to sink in and process without imposing your own thoughts or edits.

Demonstrating understanding: One of the best ways to build trust and establish rapport with your actors and creative team while actively listening is to verbally and non-verbally demonstrate understanding of the message. One method to verbally demonstrating understanding is to encourage the speaker with affirmations like "I see," "I understand," or "Interesting," as appropriate. A method to reinforce clarification is to paraphrase the speaker's idea. By repeating what the speaker has just said, rather than thinking about what you want to say next, you will be communicating that you have actually received the speaker's message.

Summarizing her philosophy of active listening when directing, West coast director Kate Danley shared: "It is my job to let my actors know they are safe so that they can then open up and be emotionally vulnerable to each other." On describing her rehearsal setting, she added:

> I say to my actors to let me know if something feels awkward or if they have an idea, and I take all of their suggestions enthusiastically. We try everything out first before deciding whether it works or not. I believe acting should be playful and joyful . . . .

Her working environment certainly sounds collaborative, where active listening is key, wouldn't you agree? As stated previously, active listening involves concentrating on the speakers' messages and letting them know their messages are being heard. As in Kate's example, active listening also involves being open to accepting suggestions "enthusiastically." Additionally, demonstrating understanding either verbally, non-verbally, or both is an important active listening technique. Finally, you can build trust, encourage further collaboration, and demonstrate understanding by using open-ended questioning to ask for clarification – an additional technique to active listening.

Open-Ended Questioning and Responses

Questioning is a common communication tool that directors use in all four group dynamics stages. As an active listening technique, open-ended questioning is vital in both clarifying the speaker's message and encouraging further response. As a starting point in rehearsal, by focusing on open-ended questions, you can pursue deeper, more mindful responses from your actors to bring your concept to life. With your creative team, you can demonstrate your understanding and encourage collaboration by utilizing open-ended questions as well. It is important that the entire ensemble as well as the director participate in open-ended questioning. By modeling this type of questioning, a director can go a long way in creating the desired effect.

Generally, open-ended questions are those that require more than a simple, one-word answer. These require the responder to pause, reflect, and think deeply. The answers will not necessarily be based on facts, but rather personal feelings, ideas, creative images, or opinions. In production meetings and rehearsals, where your goal is to work toward a creative environment, open-ended questions and responses are essential for developing strong characters, getting to the essence or spine of the play, and plugging into your concept for the production.

Begin by using language that promotes thoughtful responses. Ask "how," "why," and "what" questions. When working in response to your actors' or creative team's feedback, begin your probes with "I wonder . . .," "What do you think . . .," "Have you considered . . .," or "What would happen if . . .?" Using this type of questioning will not only show your actors and creative team that you value their input, but will also open the door to additional suggestions, ideas, and action on their part. Experiment with this type of leading questioning at your next production meeting or rehearsal and see how the results begin to change.

As a starting point, open-ended responses from the director will also strengthen the positive working environment. Rather than qualifying rehearsal choices with "great choice" or "that's not working," look for open-ended responses like "interesting choice" or "I see where you're going with that choice." Why? When the director constantly compliments a couple of actors about their choices to the exclusion of others, the work environment can begin to feel less inviting and creativity suffers. A simple re-thinking of how you use questions and responses will help immensely.

Elizabeth van den Berg, theatre professor at McDaniel College near Baltimore, Maryland, stated that her stance when collaborating with both her actors and creative team is to "take the Socrates approach" and focus on questioning, with an interesting twist. "I try to follow the improvisation rule of 'Yes, and . . .' whenever possible," she shared. In the classic improvisation scene played with a partner, the idea is that both actors never say no to any line thrown at them. For example, once established that you are on a deserted island, you don't say, "No, we're on Times Square." You must add to the scene with the line "Yes, and . . ." – for example, "Yes, and those coconuts look exquisite!" The other actor's job is to build upon that line. Professor van den Berg does caution that "ultimately the director must ensure that the production fulfills the needs of the script, so knowing when to say 'no' is also helpful." As a young director, you may want to incorporate "Yes, and . . ." in addition to questioning as a way to keep your own collaborative process open and fruitful.

Another approach is to end rehearsal with a thoughtful review of questioning, not only about text and character specifics, but about the process. Hamilton Clancy, Artistic Director of The Drilling Company in New York City, recommends: "Always ask at the end of every rehearsal: What did we learn? Keep asking questions. Learn to practice a life of non-judgment and acceptance of others." In this way, Hamilton has kept the channels of communication open with his acting company and created a framework for collaborative theatrical work.

While these are great examples of opening up dialogue in an effort to create a foundation for a collaborative rehearsal hall and production meeting, remember that you are still the director and your vision and clarity are vital. You will need to find the balance between openness and firmness. As Noah Himmelstein, Associate Artistic Director of Everyman Theatre in Baltimore, Maryland offers: "I work to create a very open room where actors can contribute their ideas, point of view, and feel willing to risk looking foolish. I am decisive when needed in order to maintain the direction we're going in . . . ." Noah maintains focus on the spine of the play and uses this to guide his creative team and actors. He adds:

> I welcome input – most likely I'll be inspired in ways I never would have imagined on my own, but I do need to be clear and decisive when necessary, i.e. cutting something a designer has worked on or may advocate fiercely for but my gut says doesn't help tell the story in the end.

Being strong, decisive, and learning to say "No" may be difficult, especially in the beginning. I recommend heeding Noah's advice and returning to your concept for guidance whenever a potential conflict occurs. This is exactly what I needed to do with a lighting designer I highly respected during a production of Aurand Harris' *Punch and Judy* for Western Maryland College in Westminster, Maryland. Aesthetically, the concept called for starkness for this play filled with bizarre puppet characters including the violent Punch and Judy, a Devil, and ghoulish ghosts. The set involved a puppet stage draped in mesh fabric inside a Victorian toy theatre framed with footlights. We experimented with no gels on the footlights, creating harsh light on the actors' faces and shadows, but certainly in line aesthetically with the concept. I suggested the entire production be lit in the same vein. The lighting designer, however, had planned a colorful, rather playful light plot, zeroing in on the puppet theme rather than the cruel harshness of the concept. In this case, we returned to the concept as the guide for the production. After much discussion and collaboration, the lighting designer reworked the design to retain that harshness. While I'm not suggesting that directors should tell their designers how to do their jobs, there may be rare instances when you need to check in with your concept and make sure the design elements are on track.

You may need to check in with yourself at times and ask: Have I been listening actively and openly to my creative team; or have I been asserting my own ideas too often? Have I allowed my actors the space they need to provide input, to experiment and create freely during rehearsals; or have I dictated every moment of the play? Have I asked open-ended questions both as a listening technique for clarification and as a directing tool to explore, or have I abandoned these strategies? Have I trusted the text and the concept to lead the way: or have I faltered, lost my way, become distracted? Maintaining balance between the open, collaborative working environment and remaining true to the aesthetic/historical/cultural concept you envision requires not only mastery of the communication skills already discussed, but also leadership skills. Do you consider yourself a strong leader? What are some characteristics of a good leader? What are some specific leadership qualities necessary in the directorial process?

Incorporating Leadership Skills in Managing the Collaborative Theatre Environment

Disciplined, fair, respectful, mindful, motivational, compassionate – these are characteristics I hear over and over that describe a strong leader. When reflecting on the best directors I have worked with in the past, these characteristics also apply. As a young director, you must be aware that mastering staging technique and communication skills are only part of your journey. Developing leadership skills requires constant self-reflection, time, and energy, but will make you a better director.

Strong leaders are *disciplined and fair*. As director Kate Danley described earlier, a director is the leader and must set the example for both cast and crew by demonstrating an excellent work ethic, respect, and fairness. She encourages directors to "Praise those who are doing well, and address the issues that arise calmly, fairly, and swiftly." What kind of leader will you be when faced with tough artistic decisions, administrative crises, or personnel issues? For example, in the academic theatre environment where these issues fall under the director rather than the stage manager or production manager, will you tolerate lateness to rehearsal, or is that a "let it slide" issue? How many times will you tolerate lateness? What happens when the rest of your cast notice that it's okay to show up late? What about no-shows to rehearsal? Will you tolerate that? How will you demonstrate to the cast "calmly, fairly, and swiftly" that you have a certain tolerance for these behaviors in rehearsal? Will you state some rehearsal policies at the first rehearsal meeting, or are you afraid that your cast won't like you if you come across too hard in the beginning? Is there a middle ground? Showing respect as well as a fair and disciplined approach to your rehearsal policies and procedures is part of the leadership expected of a director in these non-professional environments.

One of the biggest obstacles student directors face is finding that middle ground between being in charge and being a peer when working on lab directing projects. Avoiding this potential pitfall can prevent the demise of the entire production. Being aware of common stumbling blocks ahead of time can give you an opportunity to develop a strategy for dealing with cast and production team issues. Table 3.1 lists several common rehearsal or production issues that may arise and ways that communication and leadership can be used to resolve these issues.

A strong leader is *respectful*, and often this requires some introspection to ask yourself how you handle interactions with your actors in the

Table 3.1 Rehearsal/production issues and communication/leadership resolutions

Issue	Resolution
Actors taking advantage of the rehearsal schedule/director	Communicate expectations. • Restate rehearsal policies and define changes as needed, including a penalty if policies are not complied with. Lead by being prepared to follow through.
Actors either bored or frustrated	Self-reflect on your rehearsal organization: • Are you calling actors to rehearsal who don't need to be there? • Are you unprepared for rehearsal? Lead by making personal changes: • Pledge to respect your actors' time and effort.
One actor abusing the schedule/ other actors are angry	Communicate first with the problem actor. Next, lead by addressing the entire cast to let them know the steps you've taken. • However, handle the situation delicately. You don't want the entire cast to turn on the actor and cause any more division.
One actor not doing his/her job/needs to be replaced	Communicate first with the problem actor. • Have a plan/timeline for replacement. Lead by addressing the entire cast, delicately. Again, you don't want to create any more division amongst the cast.
Creative staff not doing their part/ communication issues	Encourage communication by all means available: email, text, phone, meetings. If the problems persist, lead by developing a plan for replacing problem creative staff as necessary.
Tech rehearsal nightmares	The more pre-planning and discipline on your part, the smoother tech will be. • Insist on a paper tech where potential tech issues can be communicated. Assert your leadership skills where necessary.

rehearsal studio or your creative team during production meetings. For example, in the rehearsal studio, do you have a plan in place for praising those who are doing well, or are your notes primarily focused on the negative? On the other hand, how will you compassionately balance that praise so the entire cast feels encouraged? How will you address issues that seem to disrupt your rehearsal process? Have you created a collaborative framework to positively work out these types of issues? For example, what happens when ideas clash in the rehearsal hall? As the artistic director of a theatre company committed to producing new plays in New York City, Hamilton Clancy is experienced in working with actors as they explore and analyze the meaning behind these new works in a collaborative fashion. He reflects: "Every so often [actors] will have an idea that I'm not crazy about or vice versa and we have to try on each other's shoes until we decide which one will work best for the show." In these cases, active listening and open-ended questioning may be useful in the rehearsal studio as well as experimentation – a classic example of respectful collaboration between director and cast.

Strong leaders use a *mindful* approach to the directing process, whether working in an academic environment, a professional theatre, or somewhere in between. Mindfulness in your process will go a long way in managing your collaborative atmosphere. Mindfulness as a director includes periodic self-reflection and assessment and the willingness to accept responsibility when things go awry. As a director applying mindfulness to the rehearsal hall, do you take time to self-reflect, accept responsibility for your own communication misunderstandings, and make adaptations as necessary? In the rehearsal studio, are you willing to accept ownership of artistic risks, and can you admit if an idea has backfired? Can you learn from the mistake and move in another direction? Leadership requires mindful risk-taking, courage, and adaptability.

A great tool to help develop a mindful approach to rehearsals (or the pre-production stage) is the use of a directing journal. The journal's use can be adapted to suit your personal needs, but I've outlined a potential guideline below:

1) Prior to the rehearsal (or a production meeting), jot down the goals for the rehearsal session (or meeting) in terms of what you would like to cover. Next, jot down your personal goals in terms of what skill(s) you would like to master. For example, your pre-rehearsal journal entry may look like this:

   Rehearsal goal: Quick blocking review of Act 1, scenes 1–4 followed by character/relationship questions and discussion

   Personal goal: Improve listening and questioning skills to encourage collaboration with acting ensemble

2) After rehearsal, take some time to reflect on both the goals, asking yourself where you succeeded and where you may need to continue to work. Reflect on the communication skills that may help you, on which group dynamics stage the ensemble may be experiencing, or on warmups, theatre games, or exercises that may enhance the rehearsal process.

3) Jot these ideas down in your post-rehearsal reflection, which in turn will help you set your goals for the next rehearsal.

The director's journal can be a helpful tool for mindful self-reflection beyond the academic theatre lab. As you are expanding your directing resume, you will be working with new groups of actors and creative personnel. A director's journal is a good place to continue to reflect, self-assess, re-group, and change direction, if necessary.

Strong leaders *motivate* and are able to inspire others with ease. Directors use motivation with their casts and creative teams to bring positive results during the rehearsal process and in production meetings. These methods of motivation include:

1) Finding ways to inspire
2) Assessing and changing direction
3) Being a role model
4) Instilling hope and encouragement, not fear
5) Being attuned to actors/creative team

To *inspire your ensemble*, you yourself must be inspired and demonstrate your excitement for the project to your ensemble. First, love the play you are directing. You will be living with this text for a long time, so you must find it stimulating, challenging, endearing, and sustaining. Next, you'll need to do the preparation work so that you can inspire others to join the journey. If you have taken your preparation work seriously, analyzed the play for aesthetic/historical/cultural emphasis, considered how the play relates to today's audience, and developed an exciting concept/vision, you are ready to inspire your actors and creative team. You will inspire them by telling the story of your vision of this play. Challenge your ensemble to join you on this journey and let them know that you believe in their unique talents for this project. Your enthusiasm will inspire and build enthusiasm.

Directors who are willing to *assess a rehearsal situation and change direction* quickly are demonstrating motivation skills. For instance, at the beginning of rehearsal, you can assess the overall mood of the actors. If everyone is exhibiting high energy and bouncing off-the-walls, consider starting rehearsal with a focus activity to redirect their energy. On the other hand, if you notice that several creative team members are not contributing during a meeting and are sitting back with arms crossed and

heads down, simply ask for their feedback on a specific point or introduce a brainstorming activity to draw them back into the conversation,
if appropriate for your theatre setting. These types of assessments and
responses will help to move the project forward with new enthusiasm.

A motivating director will serve as a *role model*, demonstrating
respect, discipline, and emotional balance both in the rehearsal hall and
during production meetings. As discussed throughout this guide, being
prepared by fully analyzing the play and developing a concept demonstrates respect to your ensemble. Modeling respect for all personnel in
the production – actors, designers, and crew – sets a similar expecta-
tion for those around you. Keeping negative emotions in check is vital to
the health of the project. It is never appropriate for the director to have
a "melt-down," take frustrations out on the cast or crew, or otherwise
demonstrate anger toward any member of the ensemble.

Along the lines of maintaining emotional balance, a director motivates
best by *instilling hope and encouragement rather than fear*. Therefore,
using positive statements rather than threats will be more beneficial and
inspirational in the rehearsal studio or production meeting. Here is an
example of feedback after a rocky run-through of Act I:

> Instead of: "You actors should have had Act I down by now!"
>
> Try: "We've smoothed out several moments in Act I, let's focus
> on . . . ."

Or, during a production meeting with the set designer on a potential set
change issue:

> Instead of: "I've asked for something different here, but you're not
> giving me what I want!"
>
> Try: "I really like how this platform moves into place, creating a
> mountain effect in the Act I transition. Could we do something simi-
> lar during this change?"

A positive approach will always instill more confidence in your ensemble
as well as demonstrate respect and, in the long run, produce better results.

Being attuned to your individual actors as they journey through a project is another way a director leads through motivation. Artistic Director
Noah Himmelstein suggests that "timing is everything" when it comes to
leading and guiding actors:

> So much of directing is being attuned to each individual actor's pro-
> cess . . . . It may be there is something that comes clear very early
> on but the actor isn't ready to hear it then if they are just starting

to make sense of the text; but if saved for say the third week of the process, could open up the mysteries of an entire play and allow for deeper work for the remainder of the process.

Learning to become attuned to your actors' needs is a sign of directorial leadership. Whether this means revealing information as actors are ready or knowing when to take an early break because your actors are fatigued, this is a skill that you will acquire over time, but starts with observation and awareness. It requires patience and restraint on your part, but as Noah describes, deepens the process overall.

Finally, strong leaders are *compassionate*. Nothing demonstrates compassion in a strong leader/director better than the following story about a wonderful community theatre director I knew at the School of Fine Arts in Willoughby, Ohio early in my acting career. Artistic Director Gwen Yarnell demonstrated respect for actors at every audition she held, but this particular example has stayed with me for over forty years. The auditions for the musical *Brigadoon* required actors to sing sixteen bars of a show tune for the first phase of the audition. As is usual for a community theatre audition, there were all levels of auditionees, from beginners auditioning for the first time to veterans who had been in many productions.

At this particular community theatre, all of the auditionees sat in the theatre and watched the auditions, which made the newbies even more nervous. One young woman got up to sing her song and completely froze. The entire theatre started whispering and clucking, which only made matters worse for the poor woman. Gwen patiently asked the accompanist to begin again, but the woman started and froze again. This is when Gwen's compassion went into overdrive.

Gwen slowly walked up onto the stage, gently held the women's hand and talked quietly to her. She then signaled to the accompanist, and both Gwen and the woman began to sing the tune together. After a bit, Gwen stopped singing, allowing the woman to finish the song by herself. By this time, everyone in the theatre was rooting for the woman and applauded her victory. I recall applauding for Gwen's kindness as well. This was truly a moment of theatre collaboration.

Conclusion

You now have an understanding of how to begin to manage the collaborative theatre environment using exercises, theatre games, and communication tools to enhance your relationship with your ensemble. Your cast and creative team will be proceeding through the four stages of group dynamics: Forming, Storming, Norming, and Performing. By recognizing each stage, you can assist in the ensemble's smooth transition. You also have three basic communication tools for both the rehearsal hall and the production conference room – brainstorming, active listening, and questioning. While it will take time to master these communication skills, they will go a long way toward your development as a successful director and motivational leader. You understand that leadership requires discipline, fairness, respect, mindfulness, motivation, and compassion. The next chapter provides a case study of the principles outlined in Chapters 1–3, giving you an opportunity to see how they are synthesized in an actual production.

Activities for Self-Reflection

Using your journal, respond to the following prompts relating to the concepts introduced in the preceding chapter:

1) Think of a group you've joined, a production you've been involved in, or even a class at the beginning of the semester. Trace and describe the progression of the group dynamics stages: Forming, Storming, Norming, and Performing.
2) Think about what you would like your cast to take away from the first rehearsal of a current or future directing project. What activities would you introduce to help establish your specific tone for this project? How will this help ease your cast through the Forming Stage?
3) In what ways will you be working toward building a safe and trusting rehearsal environment for actors in your next directing project? In addition to the exercises and activities included in this chapter, what other activities might you use to ease your cast through the Storming Stage?
4) How do you feel about using improvisation to help your actors with character development and character objectives or to work through beats within the play? How might you use this tool once your actors feel comfortable and safe (Norming Stage)?
5) Make a list of three ways you may use the following communication skills for a collaborative theatre environment in your next production:

   a   Brainstorming
   b   Active listening
   c   Questioning

6) Describe a time you've demonstrated leadership next to each leadership quality listed:

   a   Disciplined
   b   Fair
   c   Respectful
   d   Mindful
   e   Motivational
   f   Compassionate

Don't be afraid to return to your journal and review your responses as you work through this guide. Feel free to add new insights and perspectives as you continue to evolve and grow as a person and a director.

Notes

1 Forming, Storming, Norming, and Performing: Understanding the Stages of Team Formation. *MindTools*, www.mindtools.com/pages/article/newLDR_86. htm. Accessed February 6, 2019.
2 Boal, Augusto. *Games for Actors and Non-Actors.* Translated by Adrian Jackson. Routledge, p. 78.
3 Boal, p. 75.
4 Olsen, Alex F. *Applied Imagination: Principles and Procedures of Creative Problem-Solving.* 1953. Scribner, 1979.
5 Brainstorming: Generating Many Radical, Creative Ideas. *MindTools*, https:// www.mindtools.com/brainstm.html. Accessed March 25, 2019.

Chapter 4

Synthesizing the Principles
A Case Study

The following case study synthesizes the directorial principles you have read about in the previous chapters and provides examples of communication and leadership skills throughout the Preparation, Pre-Production and Rehearsal Phases of a production of *I Never Saw Another Butterfly*. I have specifically chosen an example from an educational theatre experience to share for this guide. Why? Because for many of you these principles may apply to the productions you direct early in your career, particularly non-professional, resume-building projects. For example, if you are hired to direct a New Play festival at a small non-Equity theatre, you may also find yourself faced with a group of eager volunteers looking to you for leadership in the set, lights, and costume design. While you may need to employ more managing aspects of your directing skills in this situation, you will still want to create a positive working environment, encouraging collaboration. Let's review the case study scenario to see how these directorial principles, communication and leadership skills synthesize in an actual production scenario.

In 2004 I directed a production of the Holocaust play *I Never Saw Another Butterfly* at Winters Mills High School in Westminster, Maryland. I selected this play for both its educational appeal and its possibilities for collaboration. These collaborators included student actors, designers, and crew as well as other faculty and guest experts, making this an excellent multi-disciplinary project. This case study of *I Never Saw Another Butterfly* demonstrates the analysis of a play for aesthetic, historical, and cultural emphasis, the discipline of research and preparation, the communication of concept, the successes and struggles during the production, and the leadership skills utilized as described throughout this guide. Following the three phases of the play's development – Preparation, Pre-Production, and Rehearsal – while focusing on the director's characteristics, principles and skills, I will illustrate how all these elements merge.

Synopsis of *I Never Saw Another Butterfly*

Celeste Raspanti's *I Never Saw Another Butterfly* tells a story of real children who endured the horrors of living in the Terezin ghetto near Prague, a holding area for those who would eventually be sent to Auschwitz to be gassed. Of the 15,000 children living in Terezin, only 100 survived by the time it was liberated. Despite these difficult facts, the play reveals a hopeful message. Through the efforts of their teacher, Irena Synkova, the children learn to express their fears, hopes, frustrations, and pain through art, song, and poetry, thereby filling their short lives with dignity and strength. The pictures and poems left behind and hidden by the children have become documented proof of many of the crimes of the Nazi officers and soldiers.

The story is narrated by a young girl named Raja, whose character steps in and out of the action as scenes unfold. We meet her family just before their home is raided by Nazi soldiers and they are separated and forced into the ghetto. We share Raja's heartbreak as each family member is carried away by the train to Aushchwitz. We follow her journey as she adjusts to life at the camp in Terezin, learns to trust her teacher, and struggles to express hope again.

Preparation Phase: Research the 1940s/ Holocaust/Trip to Holocaust Museum

During my *initial exploration* for the Winters Mill High School production of *I Never Saw Another Butterfly*, I began by reading the play several times for aesthetic, historical, and cultural context. With a notebook nearby, I scored my notepad into three columns: Questions/Historical-Cultural/Images-Keywords. After each reading, the lists under each column grew. I noted questions I had about Jewish culture and listed words that were new to me as well as items that required further research. Under Historical-Cultural, I recorded specific areas I wanted to research, including: information about the history of Terezin, a map of Terezin, photos of Terezin, information about the children of Terezin, the artwork by the children of Terezin, music and art of the Holocaust in general, articles about spiritual resistance, photographs of clothing of the 1940s specifically in Prague, articles about fashion under the occupation in 1940s Europe, and photographs of homes/home goods from the 1940s. Under Images-Keywords, I jotted down any image, recurring word, symbol, or theme that jumped off the page or popped into my mind as I read and re-read the play. This column generally becomes the seed of my concept or vision of my productions. (Note: This particular approach to developing a concept is described in detail in Appendix A, "Developing a Production Concept".)

I researched the playwright, Celeste Raspanti, a specialist in Holocaust drama. In addition to *I Never Saw Another Butterfly*, Raspanti wrote *No Fading Star* and *The Terezin Promise*, two plays based on her firsthand knowledge of visiting camps, working with oral histories and her friendships with Holocaust survivors.[1] Research about the playwright was a strong endorsement that this play was honest and authentic.

In reading the script for performance concerns, I had to consider the physical requirements of the play. The script describes the staging as "An open stage . . . The stage is set with various levels and steps."[2] The actual worlds represented are Irena's makeshift school in Terezin, Raja's home in Prague, and common areas in the Terezin camp used for different situations. Rather than use abstract platforming with steps, I chose to define Raja's childhood home (symbol of hope) on a platform at stage right and Irena's art room in Terezin (symbol of hope within the hate) on a platform at stage left. I needed each platform to be multi-leveled for ease of entry by Raja as she stepped into the scene. I created an informal ground plan with entrances and exits, minimal furniture needs, and scene requirements to be shared with my student set crew and technical director.

Another consideration was the play's dual acting style, requiring both Presentational and Representational from the main character Raja. At times Raja speaks directly to the audience, narrating her story and memories (Presentational). This narration leads into a scene, and Raja enters and interacts with characters realistically (Representational). Raja is the only character in the play employing this duality – it is her story. As such, I would need to find an extraordinary high school actor for this role.

In a unique effort for a high school production, I was able to *coordinate* a field trip to United States Holocaust Museum in Washington, DC for theatre, art, music, and language art students. The student actors and crews used this event as field research, enabling them to view specific details for set, props, costumes, and individual characterization. It became the catalyst for an authentic connection to the heart of our production of *I Never Saw Another Butterfly*. While an ensemble field trip is a rare opportunity for most casts and crews to experience, I was also able to purchase two books that included prints of the Terezin children's artwork and poetry. And the internet provides virtual tours of many locations and collections from museums, bringing field research closer to home.

After multiple readings and much research, a central concept for *I Never Saw Another Butterfly* began to solidify. A review of my list of images from the readings plus notes from the field trip led me to a production concept of Symbols of Hate and Hope. I was excited to see how I could *empower* and *guide* the creative team as well as the actors to artistically express this concept.

The field trip as well as a few additional special rehearsal sessions to assist the actors, which I will detail later, had to be considered in my *scheduling* as I laid out the pre-production meeting and rehearsal schedule for the production. For instance, we were working on a five-week rehearsal schedule prior to tech week, rehearsing two hours a day, generally three days a week. Bringing in special guests to work with the actors on Jewish culture or Czech pronunciation meant I needed to make up for that lost rehearsal time by adding a fourth rehearsal day on those weeks. I always like to build in one or two extra rehearsal days in case we get behind, especially when working on the high school level.

Pre-Production Phase: Communication of the Overall Concept/Spine

In the high school setting, I design the basic set, costumes, lights, etc. and assign a student coordinator in each area to help bring it to fruition. It is my job to communicate the overall production concept as clearly as possible and then *empower* the coordinator and crew to contribute ideas. I am available to *advise* and troubleshoot, and *coordinate* resources as necessary.

The set for *I Never Saw Another Butterfly* encompassed three main acting areas: Raja's family's apartment in Prague prior to the raid by Nazi soldiers, Irena's art room for the children in Terezin, and a general area representing multiple other locations. As mentioned earlier, I decided to make the worlds of Raja's family apartment and Irena's art room less abstract by devoting physical space at each side of the stage. At the *pre-production meeting*, it was my task to communicate the aesthetic as well as the historical and cultural aspects of the play and how these relate to the overall concept. I shared photos of the 1940s as well as articles from my research about Terezin and field work from the United States Holocaust Museum in Washington, DC to represent both the symbols of hate and hope – the key to the concept. The student design coordinators were completely onboard and *ideas* for set dressing and costume elements began to *flow freely*. The set coordinator and crew pulled furniture and set dressings to outfit both the apartment and art room spaces, and we collaborated on suggestions for stage painting techniques for the flats attached on each platform – concrete bricks for the art room and a textured effect for the apartment. Additionally, the unit set incorporated the "Arbeit Macht Frei" ("work sets you free") slogan which appeared at the entrance of Auschwitz and other Nazi concentration camps. The crew created a brick wall upstage with the gate and arched sign "Arbeit Macht Frei," a looming symbol of hate that remained dimly lit throughout the play. Using *brainstorming*, the set coordinator and crew were able to problem-solve an issue with how to best utilize the stage extensions on either side of the main performing stage. Using the concept as their guide, they devised a symbolic effect to frame the main stage on either side with dimly lit barbed wire fencing, created by wooden poles, wire, and strategically placed twist ties. They added, piles of shoes and empty suitcases under the fencing, more symbols of the hate and destruction imposed on so many lives as their belongings were left at train stations during the Holocaust. The use of brainstorming with the set coordinator and crew resulted in a concept-driven solution to our problem.

While I *guided* the general design and building of the set, lights, costumes, and properties for the production, the theatre students at Winters Mill High School collaborated on the execution in every aspect. For example, I provided copies of my research of fashions of the 1940s to the student head of the costumes, and *empowered* her to discuss options with her crew of student volunteers. Together we discussed the historical aspects of the costumes of this era, and she did additional research on her own. After pulling possible costumes from the school's collection and supplementing with a trip to Goodwill, the head of costumes reconvened with me to articulate her costuming ideas for each character. Based on her initial assessment, I *advised* which costumes needed to be built or rented. These advising sessions, where *questioning, active listening*, and *brainstorming* strategies were employed, provided many opportunities for the creative coordinators to input their own ideas and take ownership. That's not to say that I never vetoed an idea, but my rule of thumb was to return to the concept for guidance.

One example of great problem-solving that emerged from the *questioning, active listening, brainstorming* strategy concerned a costuming issue for the six children brought to the Irena's underground school. After the advising session, the costume crew designed a wonderful, inexpensive solution. We needed a costume change to show that these six children were now part of the school, but couldn't afford a complete costume change for six actors. Using stock fabric, the student costumers created simple smocks that slipped over the head and unified the group of children.

After clarifying the concept with the student props master, the team created a list of props that reflected both symbols of hate and hope. On the one hand, they were required to find all the shoes and suitcases to dress the sides of the stage; on the other hand, they created the colorful artwork of the children of Terezin that was continually added to the set as the play progressed, symbolizing the children's growing courage and hope. This prop artwork was based on the actual artwork the students saw at the United States Holocaust Museum or from the reference books, not just some childlike painting they created. They also researched and created Jewish Sabbath candles for Raja's home in the opening scene and a ritual wedding canopy, both representing hope for Raja's family during a very dark time.

Similar collaboration occurred with the student lighting and sound effects coordinators. After describing the overall concept of Symbols of Hate and Hope and sharing my research of photographs and initial sketches, I could tell these team members were on board. It was the perfect environment to *empower* my creative team to come up with creative solutions to artistically express this concept. For instance, for a positive symbol at the end of the play, the lighting designer used a butterfly gobo, a metal stencil that is placed in front of a light source to project an image. This butterfly image appeared at the final moment of the play to symbolize the message of hope that Irena had passed along to her young charges despite the dark, ugly hatred they had been forced to experience at Terezin. The lighting coordinator came up with an effective light cue whenever the Nazi soldiers entered. By mounting four scoops gelled in red on the floor behind the upstage wall, the scoops would shine against the cyclorama, creating a powerful harsh effect. Finally, the student sound effects coordinator researched a number of important sounds used throughout the play, such as a haunting train whistle representing more victims being whisked away to a concentration camp. While these may seem like basic scenic design skills, the broader point is that in this particular theatre environment, the results evolved through collaboration and were guided by a concept.

In addition to collaborating with my student creative team, the arts faculty at Winters Mill High School were also engaged in *I Never Saw Another Butterfly*. The music which played throughout *I Never Saw Another Butterfly* was carefully selected to represent either the Jewish tradition, authentic life in Terezin, or national Czechoslovakian roots. Dvorak is a Czech composer, and I used his *Slavonic Dances* to represent Raja's family ties to their homeland, while *Supplication* by Bloch played during the Sabbath Prayer. The children's opera *Ludvik* was meant to represent the beloved *Brundibar*, which was historically performed in Terezin many times with a child cast. I chose two choral selections from *Brundibar* and had my actors pantomime actions to it. Winters Mill's choral teacher, Mrs. Caren Bezansen, surprised me with the discovery of a CD of the San Francisco Children's Chorus singing many of the actual Terezin children's poems, discovered at the end of World War II. I found a way to incorporate several of these songs into the play as well. I appreciated her thoughtful, spontaneous collaboration on this project. Additionally, the instrumental teacher, Ms. Kristen Gottlieb, encouraged a clarinet student to provide klezmer music in the lobby prior to each performance.

The visual art faculty also collaborated on this production, particularly with the set. Ms. Leah Spencer's drawing class created sketches of the human figure, then combined these drawings with historical research and photographs of actual concentration camp victims, based on their research from the United States Holocaust Museum field trip. Finally, they used their sketches to create life-size versions of figures from the Holocaust. These charcoal figures were then incorporated into the set design among the barbed wire fencing as a constant reminder of the fate awaiting Raja's family and all the children of Terezin. Ms. Sharon Schaefer's art students were encouraged to learn specific stage painting techniques and helped to dress the set.

There were several *casting considerations* for *I Never Saw Another Butterfly*, including the size of the cast and age range of the roles. While I welcomed the opportunity of involving as many student actors on stage as possible, as a director I must also balance the educational experience with artistic excellence and student pride of ownership. *I Never Saw Another Butterfly* offers seventeen roles with the opportunity to add extras. I added two Nazi soldiers to use in scene transitions, and an additional child in the underground school at Terezin, bringing the total number of roles to twenty.

Raja, the lead role, was tricky because it required an actor who could handle many monologues, move with ease between representational and presentational acting, and show emotional depth. Raja is a child whose dear family are ripped away from her and finds herself in Terezin, the Nazi holding camp. This role requires sensitivity and range. I took a chance and cast a freshman and newcomer to theatre. Sometimes a director has to trust the gut. Irena, the teacher of an underground school in Terezin, befriends Raja and develops a close relationship. I cast a senior and veteran theatre student as Irena. This combination resulted in a beautiful, balanced energy.

The play required six additional young people listed only as Child I, Child II, etc. in the List of Characters. I needed to look for physically smaller actors who could pass as children. Conversely, there were several older characters – Raja's Mother, Father, Aunt, and the Rabbi – each requiring a more mature stage and vocal presence. Based on these character requirements, I needed to prepare the audition material according to younger and older character types. I wrote up short descriptions of each character as well as a synopsis of the play to post on the call board along with the audition information so that the auditionees were aware of the range of roles available. I also made the script available on a sign-out basis for students interested in preparing for their auditions by learning more about the roles available. This was particularly important because *I Never Saw Another Butterfly* was not a well-known play. (Note: On the professional level, actors will seek out the script and do everything possible to prepare for an audition; on the academic level, we encourage actors to do so.)

In *coordinating* the auditions for *I Never Saw Another Butterfly*, I chose three approaches – monologues from the play, short scenes from the play, and theatre games. Knowing the physical types needed for each character and having several short monologues/scenes pre-selected helped to save time during the auditions. Since the actors playing the children roles needed to have child-like innocence, I prepared two theatre games to help me filter those auditionees. I was looking for energy, creativity, and youthfulness during the theatre games, which I rated on the actors' audition forms under the "Imagination" category.

At the actual audition for *I Never Saw Another Butterfly*, actors indicated which role(s) they were interested in on the audition form. In the educational or youth theatre environment, even if I don't envision that particular actor in the role, I always honor these reading requests as this helps the actor grow. And often I'm surprised at the result and change my preconceived thoughts about a role! For *I Never Saw Another Butterfly*, I auditioned actors in groups of six or eight, re-using and rotating the boys due to greater number of girls auditioning. I used paired scenes for the adult roles and short monologues for the child roles. I also incorporated theatre games for the group of actors I had targeted as appropriate for the children. Utilizing my personal rating system for auditions as described in Chapter 1, I made notes on the actors' audition forms about prior experience, appropriateness for the role, vocal quality, imagination, and stage presence. This system helped me to sort through the large number of auditionees and narrow down actors to call back for each role. At the call-back auditions, I re-used the paired scenes for the adult roles, but added two longer monologues for the two female leads, Raja and Irena. Also, instead of theatre games for the child roles, I added a scene where all the children are present, rotating different combinations of actors into the scene. From this process, I was able to select the cast of twenty roles needed for *I Never Saw Another Butterfly*.

A large part of casting for a high school or college program takes place before the play is even selected. What do I mean by that? I had to make sure that there were at least enough student actors available who could handle the roles in *I Never Saw Another Butterfly* before I even considered this production. Something I liked about *I Never Saw Another Butterfly* was that it only required four male speaking roles (I did add two additional Nazi soldiers for transition scenes). In the public high school setting, female auditionees generally outnumber males, so scripts that feature females are cherished. Alternately, there would have been no point in considering this play if all my strong senior actors had graduated the year before.

Rehearsal Phase: Working with the Student Actors

In order to begin to create the ideal collaborative working environment in the rehearsal hall, I began the *early rehearsals* of *I Never Saw Another Butterfly* by introducing the historical and cultural research about the

Holocaust and my overall concept of Symbols of Hate and Hope as it related to the play. I will admit that my concept was a bit fuzzy in the early days of rehearsal, but quickly came into focus after the field trip to the United States Holocaust Museum after the first week. My research served as a good introduction to our table read of the script. By sharing the photos I had collected, *asking questions* about the students' prior knowledge of the Holocaust, and *listening* to the students' responses, I was able to assess the depth of my actors' understanding and emotional commitment to the project. The *Forming Stage* began immediately for this production.

In fact, this cast quickly progressed through the *Forming, Storming, and Norming Stages* of group dynamics. For a high school cast, the group worked diligently on the tough Holocaust subject material with few distractions. As a group, the cast formed quickly, which I believe can be credited to bonding during the field trip to the United States Holocaust Museum. All of the students who attended that trip were truly moved by the experience. In addition, I used group warmups at the beginning of early rehearsals, further bonding the cast during the *Forming Stage*. The cast did have a few clashes, as I'll describe later, but overall they moved swiftly to the *Norming Stage*, where rehearsals became collaborative work sessions of *blocking and refining rehearsals*.

There were, however, a few moments within *I Never Saw Another Butterfly* when the young student actors struggled to connect with the emotional depth of the Holocaust experience, particularly during the refining rehearsals. This was understandable as these students had limited life experience and had only recently been exposed to the history of World War II and the events of the Holocaust. My job as director was to use the *refining rehearsals* to help the actors make emotional connections in whatever ways were available to them.

The heart of Raja's story in *I Never Saw Another Butterfly* is people – family, friends, a teacher, and a boyfriend – all relatable to high school students. This was the starting point as I *directed* and coached each scene and beat throughout the rehearsals. Scenes with Raja's family showing love and concern or Irena as teacher nurturing her students seemed to come together easily for the cast during the *Norming Stage* of rehearsals. However, there is an early scene where the six children first enter Terezin, frightened and unsure. This scene wasn't working because the actors really didn't have a sense of connection – what does it feel like to be children separated from their families, not sure where they are going or who they will meet there? I got up on stage with these actors and escorted them backstage to prepare for their entrance again. But before they entered, I engaged in quizzing them about their characters' backstory, *asking them questions* such as: "How many sisters and brothers do you have? Where are they now? You don't know? What happened to your Mother? Do you miss her?" They caught on immediately, and began to tell me all about their fictional families in character. I *listened and reacted with deeper questions*, weaving in historical context, as if in character myself. (Note: Every actor had completed a version of the Actor's Character Background Analysis found in Appendix C.) Next I told them that every time they made this first entrance, they needed to think about how much they missed their mothers, fathers, sisters, or brothers, and that they had no idea when they would ever see them again. I stressed that what the audience must see the moment the character walks onstage is fear, uncertainty, loneliness. By *participating* in this refining rehearsal moment, great strides were made in developing the Child roles for these actors. (Note: If this entrance had continued to be a problem, I might have engaged in a trust exercise that involved blindfolding the actors. There are several options. For ideas, refer to Augusto Boal's *Games for Actors and Non-Actors* listed in Appendix E.)

Although you have researched and prepared more than anyone else prior to rehearsals for your directing project, there may be times when you can't answer all the questions. In those cases, it's appropriate to bring in an expert. In the case of *I Never Saw Another Butterfly*, both the students and I had questions about authentic Jewish culture such as the Sabbath Prayer and the wedding which took place in the camp during the Holocaust. To accommodate these questions, I *coordinated* with the Student Government at Winters Mills High School to invite a Rabbi for student assemblies and to carve out special time for our theatre students to ask their production specific questions. To prepare for the Rabbi's visit, I had the students write down questions on index cards so that they were prepared for the expert. Their questions were insightful and demonstrated a depth of understanding of their individual characters. In addition, we were fortunate to have an exchange student from Prague at Winters Mill High School that semester, who graciously attended several rehearsals to help us with correct pronunciation of names and terms within the script. I encourage you to not be afraid to explore a variety of resources as the director.

While it may sound as though rehearsals for *I Never Saw Another Butterfly* were flawless, I can assure you that was not the case. There are times when you must assess the overall group dynamics of your cast and determine if you have a Storm on your hands. For example, what do you do when one character refuses to kiss another? When that situation arose in rehearsal for *I Never Saw Another Butterfly*, I initially thought it was simply a product of working with young actors. Thinking I was *respecting* the actor's space, I glossed over the kiss for the first two weeks of rehearsal, hoping the two actors involved would become comfortable with each other naturally. This was an error on my part because, unfortunately, the opposite occurred. Not only is it my job as director to make sure that all actors feel comfortable, but this is especially important when there is any type of intimacy occurring onstage. I needed to be much more sensitive to what I may have considered "a simple kiss." Had I addressed the moment in the script early in the blocking rehearsals, talking to the two actors involved in a sensitive manner, I would have demonstrated much more respect. In addition, the rest of the cast were becoming impatient with the two actors because this moment was slowing the momentum of the scene work. By the time I realized the actors' discomfort, I knew I had handled the situation poorly. The kiss was essential to the story and could not be cut, therefore I had to take action to remedy this situation. I began by talking to each actor individually to explore the concerns. The boy had no problem with the kiss; the girl was uncomfortable and revealed she had a boyfriend. Trying to explain that in the theatre world the kiss means nothing was getting me nowhere. In the end, I worked privately with the two actors to block a kiss that appeared real to the audience. It was the best I could do to make the young girl as comfortable as possible. Again, trying to find a solution that *respects* your actors' comfort levels and boundaries is important. I learned a valuable lesson in how to handle intimacy sensitively from this experience, which applies to high school students as well as adult actors. (Note: As with calling on expert consultants for stage combat, fencing, special effects, or dialect coaching, please be aware of the availability of intimacy directors to handle particularly intimate or violent scenes in productions you may be directing in the future. With the goal of preventing abuse or harassment of actors, incorporating trained intimacy experts is another way of demonstrating concern for *safety* and overall *respect*.)

During *tech week* for *I Never Saw Another Butterfly*, many of my leaderships skills were called into play. Being *respectful* of the actors' time while balancing the need for the technical crew to master their tasks was a balancing challenge for me during tech week. As with many productions, tensions run high during tech week, and this show was no exception. The trick was to keep a *positive attitude*, be open to a *free flow of ideas* as problems arose, and be mindful of the rehearsal goals. For instance, as the student crews' frustrations grew over scene changes not running smoothly, my job was to stay positive, but also *guide* them toward possible solutions. On the other hand, there were moments during the tech rehearsals when I needed to *manage* the timing of sound and light cues. Each directing project requires its own leadership strategies.

While there were no specific safety concerns in the actual blocking for *I Never Saw Another Butterfly*, I did need to consider the actors' *safety* during tech week. Was there enough light backstage for actors to move safely? Did dressers have room and privacy for costume changes? Were prop tables easily accessible on either side of the stage? Was all extraneous equipment, cords, cables, furniture, set pieces, etc. removed from the backstage areas? While all these tasks fall to student crew heads, in the educational theatre environment the safety of the cast and crew is my responsibility. Prior to each performance, I double checked each of these backstage safety precautions.

Finally, *leadership* by example during tech week can go a long to maintaining positive, collaborative habits. Instilling hope and encouragement, not fear or blame, can be difficult during tech week with high school students, but certainly needs to be the goal. When student actors lost focus or a crew member forgot a crucial prop, I tried to remember where they were in their own development. I encouraged respect between the actors and the crew, demonstrating appreciation with a "Thank you" and verbal recognition of a job well done.

Despite the Storm moments, the final assessment tells the whole story. The *productivity* levels of both the actors and the crew rarely waned throughout the rehearsal period. I believe the ensemble of *I Never Saw Another Butterfly* worked quickly through the four phases of group dynamics because they felt ownership of the project. Signs of working together, supporting each other, and disciplined effort let me know the group had reached the *Performing Stage*.

Conclusion

This case study synthesizes the directorial principles outlined in Chapter 1, the concepts presented in Chapter 2, and the group dynamics process, communication and leadership skills found in Chapter 3. By demonstrating specific applications throughout the Preparation, Pre-Production and Rehearsal Phases of the production of *I Never Saw Another Butterfly*, you have seen how these strategies can work together to create and manage a collaborative working environment. In Part II you will begin to practice and apply the principles illustrated above. Part II introduces three short plays and accompanying exercises where you will be asked to use a set of guiding questions to assess and work through the Preparation Phase, Pre-Production Phase and Rehearsal Phase, respectively.

Notes

1 Raspanti, Celeste. *I Never Saw Another Butterfly*. Dramatic Publishing, p. 2.
2 Raspanti, p. 7.

Part II

Application of the Guiding Questions to Three Short Plays

Introduction

Now that you have reflected on the type of director you'd like to become and understand the concepts in creating and managing a positive working environment, you are ready to practice the principles. Part II features a series of exercises asking you to apply specific guiding questions to the Preparation, Pre-production, and Rehearsal Phases of three short plays. The first exercise is theoretical in nature, asking you to read the play, prepare, and plan as if you are going to produce the play. The second play can be approached as either a theoretical or practical exercise, depending on your availability of creative team members. The third short piece requires a practical approach as you work through the Rehearsal Phase of the process with a small cast of actors.

Read the play first, then apply the guiding questions as fully as appropriate. At the end of Chapters 6, 8, and 10 you will find Activities for Self-Reflection with questions about your discoveries as you work through these exercises. Reflecting about your personal progress in your journal is of great benefit.

Chapter 5

Goggles
A Ten-Minute Play

Public reading given at Variation Projects, Baltimore, MD, June 2017.

Character Name	Brief Description	Age	Gender/Ethnicity
GRAYSON	Worn out office worker; in a rut	Adult	Female/Any
MYSTERIOUS STRANGER	A bit smug, but alluring; knows how to work a con	Adult	Male/Any

Goggles

by Jean Burgess

Scene: *At a bus stop on a street corner. There is a bench right of Center. It is after work hours, around 6:30 in the late autumn. The sun has nearly set. Street lights are beginning to create shadows.*

We hear the sound of a bus door closing and pulling away.

GRAYSON *enters running, trying to catch the bus. She is dressed in business casual, carrying a small lunch bag.*

GRAYSON

Wait, wait! (*Sound of bus further pulling away*) Great, just great. Crappiest week of my life and now I can't even get home and just stare at the four walls of my apartment for the weekend. Damn it.

A voice comes from the shadows upstage. MYSTERIOUS STRANGER *is lurking there, wearing a trench coat and exudes an alluring, yet smug air.*

MYSTERIOUS STRANGER

Psst. Look on the ground.

GRAYSON *searches for the voice.*

MYSTERIOUS STRANGER

Look on the ground – to your left.

GRAYSON *turns completely around, searching.*

MYSTERIOUS STRANGER

Look down!

GRAYSON *does and finds a pair of goggles on the ground.*

GRAYSON

What the hell? (*Asking no one in particular*) Did someone drop these goggles?

MYSTERIOUS STRANGER

(*Moving out from the shadows*) These, my friend, are not just goggles. What you are holding have amazing abilities – powers – to help you relax and enjoy life. You seem like someone who could stand to enjoy life a bit more. Am I right? Of course I'm right.

GRAYSON

I seriously doubt a pair of goggles could help someone like me do all that. (*Beat*) Could they?

MYSTERIOUS STRANGER

Try them. You'll see. Everyone's doing it. They'll take you on an amazing, magical journey. You really won't believe it, no one does at first. A virtual reality experience beyond belief.

GRAYSON

I don't know . . . I'm about the least adventurous person I know.

MYSTERIOUS STRANGER

My point exactly. Look, I'm just guessing here but . . . five days a week you wake up at six a.m., grab a bagel and coffee, run to catch the bus to an unsatisfying job in the city, where you are underpaid and underappreciated. You get home around seven with some lack luster carry-out in a soggy cardboard container that you share with your kitty. After an hour or so of TV, you crawl into bed and wash, rinse, repeat. On the weekends you go to a movie for a thrill. Am I close? Of course I am.

GRAYSON

How did you–

MYSTERIOUS STRANGER

No social life, no friends . . .

GRAYSON

I have my cat. (*Long beat*)

MYSTERIOUS STRANGER

Kitty's a biter, right?

GRAYSON

(*Confessing*) Okay. I can't even pick her up. How can you know all this about me?

MYSTERIOUS STRANGER

I see it all the time. But no worries. I have your way out. (*Pointing toward the goggles*) Try them. You'll feel relaxed, less stressed. Takes the edge off, makes your life fun again.

GRAYSON

Fun?

MYSTERIOUS STRANGER

That's right. Fun. You remember fun, don't you? When was the last time you had honest to goodness fun. And laughed – right out loud? (*Begins the spin*) Imagine if you will – a magical opportunity to escape to any place you wish. Where you can feel relaxed, or excited, or even ecstatic on a whim. The goggles can do that for you.

GRAYSON

How do they work?

MYSTERIOUS STRANGER

Ah-h. A little enchantment, a little illusion, a little voodoo—

GRAYSON

What!

MYSTERIOUS STRANGER

No. (*Chuckling*) It's augmented reality. Sounds magical, doesn't it? Come on. Try it one time. What can it hurt?

GRAYSON

Augmented reality, huh? And it's really fun? (*Debating with self*) What harm can one time do?

They move to the bench. GRAYSON *sits and* MYSTERIOUS *stands behind.*

MYSTERIOUS STRANGER

Put the goggles on your face.

GRAYSON

Put the goggles on my face. (*Does so*) Nothing's happening.

MYSTERIOUS STRANGER

Wait! Now, using your imagination, ask yourself: where would you most like to be at this moment?

GRAYSON

Geez . . . uh . . . I'm not sure. I'm not a very imaginative person. People tell me that all the time.

MYSTERIOUS STRANGER

(*Impatient*) This is an important part of the magical experience! You need to be decisive. Let's try a different tact: Where would you go on vacation, if you could go anywhere? That's an easy one.

GRAYSON

Oh. Okay. The beach. I did go to the beach once. Read a few novels. Wore lots of sunscreen, of course.

MYSTERIOUS STRANGER

Of course you did. The beach it is. Now concentrate on images of the beach. Relax and see the waves; smell the salt water; feel the California sunshine on your skin.

MYSTERIOUS *pulls a rain stick from inside trench coat, where multiple props are hanging, and creates the sounds of waves.*

MYSTERIOUS STRANGER

Hear the sound of gentle waves rippling against the shore.

GRAYSON's *body begins to relax as if laying in the sun. She reaches out trying to touch the waves. At one point, she pantomimes reaching into one hand and throwing something up into the air.*

MYSTERIOUS STRANGER

Whatever are you doing?

GRAYSON

(*In a very relaxed manner*) I'm feeding the seagulls.

MYSTERIOUS STRANGER

(*Aside*) Disgusting, filthy birds! (*To* GRAYSON) Now the waves are fading; the warmth of the sun is fading; and the sounds are fading. (MYSTERIOUS *slowly stops rain stick motion and places it back in trench coat*) Remove the goggles.

GRAYSON

(*Removing the goggles, and jumping up from seat*) Wow. That was awesome. It was truly magical. I was so relaxed, mellow. And I was there. I was really, really there.

MYSTERIOUS STRANGER

A lifelike experience. I knew you'd find it alluring.

GRAYSON

I did – awesome. Hey, did you hear that? I just described something as awesome. (*Laughs*) I never describe anything as awesome. These goggle things are amazing.

GRAYSON *begins to catch breath. Then seems perplexed. Looks at goggles in hands.*

MYSTERIOUS STRANGER

Is anything wrong? Was the experience not everything I promised it would be?

GRAYSON

Oh no, no! It was wonderful. Great. So great that now I'm even more bummed out about going home to stare at the four walls of my apartment. All I can think about is trying on the goggles again for another magical adventure.

MYSTERIOUS STRANGER

Hmm, is that so? Well, there's no reason you can't.

GRAYSON

Really?

MYSTERIOUS STRANGER

And you can go anywhere.

GRAYSON

Anywhere? Like where?

MYSTERIOUS STRANGER

Ancient Egypt.

GRAYSON

Ancient Egypt?

MYSTERIOUS STRANGER

Outer space.

GRAYSON

Outer space?

MYSTERIOUS STRANGER

Any. Where.

GRAYSON

Anywhere.

MYSTERIOUS STRANGER

Yep, anywhere you can imagine.

GRAYSON

Wow, anywhere I wish.

MYSTERIOUS STRANGER

(*Beat*) But it'll cost you.

GRAYSON

Cost me?

MYSTERIOUS STRANGER

You see, the first trip is free. After that there's a nominal fee, you understand? Of course you do. That will be fifty dollars please.

GRAYSON

Fifty dollars? That's kind of steep.

MYSTERIOUS STRANGER

Entirely up to you. (*Begins to walk away*)

GRAYSON

Wait! What the heck. I deserve it, right? (*Reaches in pocket for money and hands it over*)

MYSTERIOUS STRANGER

Whatever you say. (*Leads* GRAYSON *back to bench and stands behind*) Put the goggles on your face.

GRAYSON

(*Does so*) Goggles on.

MYSTERIOUS STRANGER

Now using your imagination– (GRAYSON *is already smiling broadly, pointing*) You see it, already?

GRAYSON

Oh yes! They're scurrying around, so comical.

MYSTERIOUS STRANGER

(*Unsure of the context, starts to pull out a butterfly net from trench coat*) Uh, well then, perhaps you'll need this . . .

GRAYSON

Now, I'm following them inside, where it's so warm and cozy.

MYSTERIOUS STRANGER

(*Puts net away, continuing to search for location clues*) Ahh . . . it's warm and cozy. And they've stopped scurrying?

GRAYSON

You bet. They are at their assigned stations now, preparing. And look at all the colors everywhere.

MYSTERIOUS STRANGER

(*Even more confused*) Assigned stations, colors everywhere, hmm. But, uh, what about that horrible smell? How would you describe that wretched odor?

GRAYSON

(*Inhaling deeply*) Oh no, it's wonderful! The sweet smell of cinnamon and fresh baked cookies. I'm sure Mrs. Claus is in the kitchen baking them herself.

MYSTERIOUS STRANGER

(*Under breath*) You're freaking kidding me! (*To* GRAYSON) Er, brilliant. (*Pulls jingle bells from among the props in trench coat*) You hear the sound of elves busying themselves at . . . (*Gagging on the word*) Santa's . . . Workshop. Holiday bliss surrounds you.

GRAYSON *is smiling, laughing, as if a giddy child, clapping hands and pointing at the virtual fantasy world unfolding.*

MYSTERIOUS STRANGER

And the images are beginning to fade . . .

GRAYSON

No, no. A little longer. Please. It's exactly like I'd always imagined – shiny new toys, elves hard at work, the smell of cinnamon and cookies—

MYSTERIOUS STRANGER

Which are all slowly fading. (MYSTERIOUS *slowly stops the bells and places them back in the trench coat.*) Remove the goggles.

GRAYSON

Wonderful. I was there, right there. But it was more than that. I felt this joy. Oh, I dunno . . . this overwhelming feeling of Christmas. Is that crazy? (*To herself*) I wonder why I stopped celebrating Christmas.

MYSTERIOUS STRANGER

Well, I'm just glad you enjoyed your illusion.

GRAYSON

Illusion? No, I was there. It was all real.

MYSTERIOUS STRANGER

Whatever you say. (*Begins to walk away*)

GRAYSON

No wait. I swear. I was at the beach and I was really at Santa's Workshop. The goggles are magical. They have magical powers of some sort.

MYSTERIOUS STRANGER

They're virtual reality goggles, that's all. The brain can't tell the difference between an actual or virtual experience. Quite alluring, wouldn't you say? Of course you would. No sorcery needed. The mind can be quite susceptible on its own, especially minds belonging to undisciplined, worn down, isolated, sad sacks.

GRAYSON

Hey!

MYSTERIOUS STRANGER

Admit it. You jumped into the hamster wheel years ago and left behind your love of Christmas and relaxing beach vacations. You're simply existing day to day. Why? Because you settled for the motto "Work and Occasionally Live" instead of "Live the Heck Outta Life." Look at you; you're exhausted.

GRAYSON

Okay, okay. But what do I do about it?

MYSTERIOUS STRANGER

You get some excitement into your life. Have you ever thought about checking out the Golden Dragons of China, or picking a coconut in the Hawaiian sunshine, or stalking an elephant on an African Safari?

GRAYSON

I did used to love the photo's of Africa in the National Geographic.

MYSTERIOUS STRANGER

Didn't we all? What's stopping you now? It's your choice. You can go to the Serengeti anytime you want.

GRAYSON

I can!

MYSTERIOUS STRANGER

Giraffe, lion, zebra.

GRAYSON

Kangaroo?

MYSTERIOUS STRANGER

Not on the Serengeti. Perhaps another trip.

GRAYSON

What about wildebeest? Oh, and monkeys?

MYSTERIOUS STRANGER

Oh you better believe it. You'll be seeing monkeys for sure. So what do you think?

GRAYSON

Yes, yes. I really want to go to Africa. (*Searching pockets for cash, but coming up empty*)

MYSTERIOUS STRANGER

No cash, no worries. (*Whips out a tablet or smartphone with a Square device for taking credit cards*) I'm equipped to take credit cards.

GRAYSON

Great. Let's do it. (*Pulling out a credit card from pocket, and signing name on device*) I'm ready for my adventure. (*Moves to the bench*)

MYSTERIOUS STRANGER

(*Standing behind* GRAYSON) Put on the goggles, and begin to imagine the sights of the Serengeti. See the landscape begin to fill up with animals freely roaming through the brush and along the water's edge. (*Pulls out a small fan from trench coat*) Feel a warm breeze through your hair. You are standing in the middle of an African wilderness. Breathe it in.

GRAYSON

(*While taking a deep breath, she reacts to her first sighting*) Oh yes, over by the tree line. A giraffe family. Look at the baby – adorable. (*Rising*) And there, by the water's edge. Zebra drinking. There must be 20, 30, maybe more. Gorgeous. Oh dear, they seem startled. (*She turns her head*) Crap! I see it. A huge lion. He's coming this way . . . He's . . . (*Whispering*) He's. Right. Here. (*Freezing, holding breath, then finally releasing*) Thank God, he saw the zebra. Whew! Wait, what's happening? The ground . . . trembling. Earthquake? God, it's a herd of wildebeest. Duck! (*She takes cover at the end of the bench, reacting to stampede*) Are they gone? Am I alive?

Note: *During the stampede,* MYSTERIOUS *places a small item on* GRAYSON's *back, which is unseen by the audience until her exit.*

MYSTERIOUS STRANGER

The images begin to fade, the sounds begin to fade, the feelings begin to fade. Remove the goggles.

GRAYSON

(*Removes the goggles, handing them to* MYSTERIOUS) Wow, that was terrifying and exhilarating and amazing. The air, the sounds, the animals. I love these adventures. (*Sound of the bus approaching*) Hey, that's the last bus. I gotta go.

MYSTERIOUS STRANGER

You sure you don't want another try? Maybe check out the kangaroos in the Outback or snorkel in the Great Barrier Reef?

GRAYSON

Wow, that sounds great. Maybe one more . . . (*A moment of struggle*) No, I can't. I really have to go.

As GRAYSON *exits, audience sees a stuffed monkey attached to her back.*

MYSTERIOUS STRANGER

(*Calling after* GRAYSON) Whenever you want the goggles again, you can find me right here. (*To self*) And you WILL be back.

MYSTERIOUS *takes out cell phone and dials.*

MYSTERIOUS STRANGER

(*Into phone*) Hey, it's me. Another one hooked . . . Yep. And I've got this one's credit card number. (*Exiting, chuckling*)

FADE TO BLACK.

Chapter 6

Application of Guiding Questions to Preparation Phase

Goggles

Instructions

This exercise is to be approached as a theoretical application. (You will work in isolation and prepare as if you are planning to direct this play. Your instructor may pair you with a stage manager for theoretical discussion purposes, as some questions do involve coordination with a stage manager.)

Now that you have read the play *Goggles*, assume that you are in the Preparation Stage of directing this production. Review and apply the following guiding questions as you analyze *Goggles* for an appropriate central concept, consider the physical requirements of the play, and prepare for auditions – the first steps a director takes with any directing project.

Parameters for the Exercise

Assume you are directing *Goggles* as part of an evening program for a local community theatre. You are preparing to collaborate with a team of volunteer designers and will be assisted by a stage manager. In this setting, you can assume that rights to the play have been taken care of by the theatre's producer, so you can freely move forward into the Preparation Phase.

Director Considerations – Preparation Phase for Goggles

1   Initial Exploration

   a   Have you read *Goggles* several times, considering aesthetic/ historical/cultural aspects of the play and jotting down any key words, phrases or images that resonate with you?

   b   When and where does *Goggles* take place? What information does the playwright provide, or does the playwright offer latitude here?

c   What mood is evoked as you read *Goggles*? Is there a certain atmosphere that comes to mind as you read the play? Jot down these ideas as you read.

d   What story are you telling as you direct this play? Describe this in a sentence or two.

e   What is the central conflict of the play? Are there universal ideas that can be drawn from this conflict?

f   What is the genre of *Goggles*? Although it deals with a serious topic, it does have some humorous lines and character situations. How will you describe the genre of the play to the creative team and the actors?

g   How would you describe the world of *Goggles* – the combination of the mood, atmosphere, setting, and the people inhabiting the play?

h   How can you connect the world of the play to today's audience?

i   Consider the style of *Goggles'* language. What does it suggest about how the play might be produced and/or acted?

j   Is the play Representational (the invisible audience is asked to peer into the life of the characters) or Presentational (the characters acknowledge the presence of the audience, even addressing them at times), or does it incorporate both styles?

k   What areas of research will help in the preparation of *Goggles*?

l   Have you ever used a virtual reality headset yourself, or observed someone using one? Regardless of your production concept, might this be important field research for this production? What other types of field or practical research have you considered?

m   As a director, do you envision a conceptual approach to the script? Use the text and your research as starting points to see if any themes, images, phrases, metaphors, or conceptual ideas come to the surface. If they do, consider how much is too much. In other words, when does concept begin to impose on a playwright's intent?

n   Once your overall concept is decided (and you've determined it is true to the spirit of the script and the playwright's intention), how clearly will you be able to communicate this vision to both the creative team and the actors?

- Can you distill your concept into a single word or phrase, or create a vivid image to convey your concept to the creative team?
- Have you considered providing photographs, illustrations, sketches, even props or music that may help convey your concept at early production meetings and rehearsals?

2   Physical Space Considerations

a   After considering the movement of the characters and possible technical issues in *Goggles*, can you envision the best physical space for the play and your concept: proscenium, thrust, Theatre-in-the-Round, environmental, or some other experimental arrangement? These are starting points to be discussed with the set designer.

b   In the case of *Goggles*, the playwright has indicated the use of a bench. How will this set piece affect your choice of space in terms of audience sightlines and in terms of any stage business?

c   What are the technical production challenges associated with each potential physical choice (i.e. lighting, set considerations are very different with a thrust or in-the-round stage versus a proscenium stage)? Have you started a list of questions to ask the creative team?

d   What is your set budget for this production? When deciding on the physical space and necessary set elements for your concept, budget is an important consideration. For example, even though the text of *Goggles* only mentions a street lamp and bench to suggest a bus stop, the set designer may envision a more realistic set with a fully painted cityscape and additional bus stop set pieces. These items would quickly increase your set budget, but if they were essential to your concept, would be worth it? How might your set budget effect your production of *Goggles*?

e   Have you created an initial sketch as a starting point for discussion with your set designer and creative team? For *Goggles*, have you determined from where the unseen bus will be approaching, entrances of the two characters, the optimal placement for the bench, and any additional set pieces that are absolutely essential to express your concept/vision for this piece? Remember this is merely a starting point for discussion with the set designer.

3   Planning/Scheduling

a   Have you determined how many weeks/number of hours of rehearsal are appropriate for a successful mounting of *Goggles*? In this community theatre setting, are you collaborating with your stage manager on the final version of the rehearsal schedule?

b   Have you considered the input of the creative team when planning for tech week rehearsals? For instance, the more technical timing required for your version of *Goggles*, the more time needed in tech rehearsal to perfect that timing.

c   Will you need any special sessions (stage combat training, dialect coaching, choreography, movement specialist, etc.) during rehearsals for *Goggles*? Make sure your rehearsal schedule allows time for specialists.

d   Has the stage manager cleared all rehearsal spaces in advance of publishing the rehearsal schedule for *Goggles*?

Activities for Self-Reflection

Using your journal, respond to the following prompts based on your experiences as you work through a theoretical Preparation Phase for a production of *Goggles*.

1   Much of the process in the Initial Exploration stage represents one style of play analysis. How is this style of play analysis similar or different from play analysis methods you've read about or used before?

2   Describe your process for arriving at your concept for *Goggles*. How do you feel your concept expresses the spine of the play and the playwright's intent? Does your concept allow the playwright's story to clearly shine through, or does it obscure the playwright's message in any way?

3   Overall, what is your impression of the director's responsibility during the Preparation Phase of a production?

Chapter 7

Deleted

A Ten-Minute Play

First Public Reading by The Actors Theatre of Grand Rapids, MI, February 2017.

Character Name	Brief Description	Age	Gender/Ethnicity
THE KEEPER	A funky young woman who keeps track of affairs in The Land of Delete	25	Female/Any
ALLEN	An unscrupulous businessman	40s	Male/Any

This play is available for instructional use free of charge. However, the publication of the play does not make it available for public performance without permission. The play is protected by copyright and may not be performed in public without the author's written permission. All paid public performances of this play are subject to a royalty. All inquiries should be directed to the playwright at jmburgess@mac.com.

Deleted

by Jean Burgess

Time: *Present*

Place: *A space defined only by stacks of files and documents of varying heights on the floor. Blurry photos and snippets of short typed messages hang from above, giving a sense that these continue vertically, upward beyond the audience's sightline.*[1]

There is a cacophony of sounds and noise: voice mail messages, scratchy video voice-overs, iTune music snippets, etc. The sound is irritating and deafening.

LIGHTS UP

ALLEN, *late 40s, in a three-piece suit is lying on the floor. Is he dead or just asleep?*

A young female, 25, is sitting on a stack of files, intently looking at ALLEN. *She's wearing a one-piece jumpsuit with a white tee shirt. Around her waist is a belt upon which is hanging a pair of headphones. She is* THE KEEPER *of this place, a custodian of sorts.*

ALLEN *begins to stir.*

KEEPER

Ah, I see you're finally getting up!

She can barely be heard over the noise.

ALLEN

Huh?

KEEPER

(*Pantomiming*) You've been out for quite a while.

ALLEN

(*Pointing to his ears*) What?

KEEPER

Ah . . . You'll need these.

She jumps off the stack of files and goes to ALLEN, *handing him a pair of headphones from the belt on her waist.* ALLEN *puts them on. Sound stops immediately for both audience and* ALLEN.

Better? (*He nods*) I was saying: Glad to see you up!

ALLEN

Where the fu— (*trying to swear, but doesn't seem to*) Where the fu—?
(*Too tired to question it, so he continues*) Where the heck am I? And who
the fu— (grunts) Who are you?

KEEPER

(*Laughing*) Oh, you're hilarious, Allen. Always plowing ahead, staying
ahead of the curve . . .

ALLEN

I really don't see what's so funny. And you don't know a thing about me
staying ahead of the—

KEEPER

(*Suddenly*) Quick duck! Incoming text!

> KEEPER *grabs* ALLEN *and pulls him down just as a text message
> comes flying in from one side of the stage, settling among the photos
> and other messages.*

ALLEN

What the fu—fu—? (*Clearly frustrated*) What was that? (*Noticing the
photos*) And what are all these . . . photos, letters? (*Allen starts reading
a fax aloud:*) To Whom It May Concern: Re: Cayman Island Account
(*Turns back to* KEEPER) I mean, what is this sh—, sh—, (*Frustrated*)
CRAP! And why can't I swear!

KEEPER

Whoa! One question at a time, mister! I can explain, if you give me half a
chance. But it might be best in small doses. Okay, here goes. This is your
Land of Delete. It's where all your deleted files, texts, e-mails, voice mails,
photos, faxes, whatever – it's where they go to live.

ALLEN

(*Looking at her strangely*) Are you freaking kidding me?

KEEPER

I assure you, I am not. Uh oh . . . incoming. Duck!

> *She grabs* ALLEN *again and yanks him down just in time as an e-mail
> flies in from off stage and settles among the photos and other hanging
> messages above.*

ALLEN

WHAT THE FU—? (*Frustrated*) And why can't I say fu—?

KEEPER

Oh that . . . I implanted a Curse Filter in you while you were out. We can't have the likes of you blurting out profanities right and left. Can you imagine the cacophony of curse words we'd have to endure. Pretty cool, huh?

ALLEN

(*Sarcastically*) Great! Now, how do I get out of this hole? (*Looking around*)

KEEPER

Oh, you can't. Once deleted; always deleted. (*Pause*) Well technically that's not true. Once in a blue moon, a file or document arrives here in The Land of Delete and some amazingly talented IT nerd is able to retrieve it – poof – (*Clicks her fingers*) like that. But you're the first actual person who's ever been deleted in his own Land of Delete.

ALLEN

The first?

KEEPER

Yep.

ALLEN

Aren't you forgetting someone? (*Pointing to her*)

KEEPER

(*Laughing*) Oh gosh, I'm not a person-person.

ALLEN

What?

KEEPER

I mean, I'm a more of a creation, a conglomerate of sorts.

ALLEN

(*Impatient*) Fine. I'll play along. And who was it that created you?

KEEPER

Well duh! That would be you. This is your Land of Delete, of course. Am I going too fast for you? I'm a conglomerate of all the people you've figuratively and literally deleted in your lifetime.

ALLEN

So that's how you know my name!

KEEPER

Now you're catching on. I'm all those "chicks" – the ones you've treated like crap, relationships you've left in shambles, minds you screwed around with, secretaries whose names you never learned.

ALLEN

Hey, it's a fast-paced world I move in, baby. I gotta take before I get taken. That's my motto.

KEEPER

Wow, you really are kind of a jerk. You never considered that one day all that taking might bite you in the butt? Or that you might be creating a kind of hell for yourself?

ALLEN

Nope.

KEEPER

Hmm, right. Well, whatever are you going to do now?

ALLEN

Well, I don't know about you, but I've got places to go, sweetheart. I'm getting out of here.

KEEPER

This oughta be fun.

She returns to the stack of files and sits. Meanwhile ALLEN crosses Right as if to exit, but hits an invisible wall. KEEPER giggles. ALLEN reacts with disgust, turns and crosses Left, but again hits an invisible wall. Now he begins to panic. He walks straight ahead Down Center, but again hits an invisible wall. KEEPER is laughing hysterically.

KEEPER

I know, I know . . . It's smaller than it looks, isn't it?

ALLEN

Wait a minute. How can this small space possibly hold all the deletes of the world?

KEEPER

Correction . . . all the deletes of YOUR world. Look up!

They both slowly look up, simultaneously.

ALLEN

Holy sh—! (*Frustrated*) Sugar!

KEEPER

Isn't it amazing?

ALLEN

No it's not amazing. It's maddening!

KEEPER

Think about it. Deleted documents and files; lost faxes and phones messages; spam; whole data bases that were supposed to be safe in the Cloud (*She chuckles at the thought*); accidently deleted photos and texts; e-mails that didn't arrived and you could never figure out why – all here in your Land of Delete. Welcome to your new home!

ALLEN

New home? Hold on! (*Jumping up and moving to the space where the text message flew in earlier*). If that text message was able to fly in here then there must be a hole of some sort. If I can just figure out where, I can get out through that hole!

He beats on the invisible wall, looking for an opening.

KEEPER

Here we go again! (*Beat*) I hate to be the bearer of bad news but there's no way out.

ALLEN

(*Continuing his desperate attempt*) You don't understand. I'm in the middle of a very important . . . uh . . . deal. What I mean is . . . I'm an important CEO. The Board of Directors can't possibly function without me.

KEEPER

(*Chuckling*) Oh, I believe they can.

ALLEN

(*Continuing his frantic search for the hole in the invisible wall*) Sorry, but you don't know a thing about big business, little missy.

KEEPER

Well, let me put it to you this way, mister. Your Board of Directors must be able to function without you because they're the ones who deleted you.

ALLEN *freezes. The realization of her words slowly sinks in.*

ALLEN

They deleted me? It can't be. They depend on me. It's just not possible. (*Beat, then complete change of tone*) Or could it? Those SOBs! How dare they do this to me! I made them millions! I put that company on the map. (*Beat, then change of tone*) That's it . . . I've got it. I'll negotiate. I'll do whatever they want if they just find a way to undelete me. They could do it, too – I'm sure.

KEEPER

I'm glad to see you're moving through the five stages of grief so rapidly. Denial, anger, bargaining . . . just zipping right through!

ALLEN

(*Distracted*) Huh? What?

KEEPER

Grief. You're working through it quickly. Good for you.

ALLEN

No I'm not. I'm developing a plan. That's what executives do, sweetie. We create and execute. Now, take a letter.

KEEPER

(*Laughing and insulted at the same time*) Oh, you are precious!

ALLEN

(*Oblivious, dictating to* KEEPER, *who simply stares at him incredulously*) Dear Henry: It appears there may have been some miscommunication (*Aside to* KEEPER) Never throw out blame in the opening of the letter – listen and learn, missy . . . (*Back to letter dictating mode*) some miscommunication in the Board's action toward me. I am still a viable asset to the team. (*Aside to* KEEPER) You see, I'm showing what a team player I am. He'll love that! (*Thinking out loud*) Let's see, terms of the negotiation – keep it short and to the point. Hmm. Ah . . . (*Back to dictating*) If the Board is willing to undelete me, I will gladly return a file I have on, shall we say some "dirty laundry," about key investors in the firm.

KEEPER

(*Holding up a file she has been sitting on*) Do you mean this file labeled "Dirty Laundry?" Apparently Chairman Henry already got wind of your little blackmail file and deleted it from your computer before you could do any damage with it. Really, Allen, you couldn't come up with a better file title than "Dirty Laundry?"

ALLEN

(*Ignoring her*) Hmm. Strange. That was top secret. Never mind . . . I'll have to resort to this. It's even better. Get this down. (*Back to dictating to* KEEPER, *who continues to ignore him*) If willing to undelete me, I will return the $7.9 million in company funds that I have hidden in an off shore account in the Cayman Islands. (*To* KEEPER) Henry would be a fool to pass up that offer!

KEEPER *jumps off stack of files and walks over to a e-mail messages hanging in the stacks.*

KEEPER

Um, I think you're a bit late on that one too, Mr. CEO! Here's a group e-mail to all the Board members that mentions the return of that money to the company. Since they've already retrieved that money, you've got no leverage, Allen.

ALLEN

What! No! It can't be. It was untraceable. The only person in the world who knew about that money was my wife. And she's dumb as a rock. There's no way she could even figure out how to communicate where it was. (*He snorts a bit*)

KEEPER

You really have an amazing respect for women, don't you?

KEEPER *sees a photo of a woman in the middle of celebration party at a restaurant among the photos hanging.*

KEEPER

By the way, is this your wife in the middle of all these suits at some restaurant called Fillini's?

ALLEN

(*Turning to look at the photo*) My God, that's her, with the Board. And that's Henry with his arm around her. And they're all smiling and laughing . . . (*Suddenly understanding*) Wait a minute!

KEEPER

Ding, ding, ding! Quickly connecting the dots, I see. (KEEPER *finds a text message and reads it aloud*) Hey, what about this text message: Are your bags packed? (*To* ALLEN) Now that sounds intriguing, doesn't it?

ALLEN

Who's that from?

KEEPER

Well, seeing how everything that lands here are your deletes and seeing how this text is from your phone, my guess is that your wife is using your phone – for the time being. The more interesting question is: who is the text to?

ALLEN

Yes, yes. Who did she send that to? And why was my wife at a restaurant with the Board of my company? (Getting increasingly upset) And why did she look so happy when clearly I've been deleted?

KEEPER *finds another photo, this one shows* ALLEN's *wife and Henry on a Hawaiian beach.*

KEEPER

Ah, I think I have found the missing link. (*Sarcastically*) Of course as a lowly female conglomerate, I may not be smart enough to put 2 + 2 together. Perhaps you should examine the evidence . . .

ALLEN

(*Snatching the photo from her*) Give me that. My God, it was her. She was the turncoat; the traitor. But I was sure she was too flighty to ever deceive me. I just didn't think she had it in her.

KEEPER

She learned from the best.

ALLEN

I've had just about enough of these wise-cracks from you.

KEEPER

Oh, you can expect a lot more of those – Remember, I'm a conglomerate of your own making: women you've screwed over and thoughtlessly deleted from your life. And truthfully, we're not real happy with you. Did you honestly think we'd be easy on you?

ALLEN

But I don't want to be stuck here with you . . .

KEEPER

Hey buddy boy, this is all your own creation, every last bit of it. Look around, look at me. Breathe it in. Welcome to your eternity. Your new home!

ALLEN

Home? This sucks.

KEEPER

Karma's a bitch, isn't it?

ALLEN

Hey, how come can you—

KEEPER

We can do or say whatever we want, Mr. CEO. Don't you love it?

ALLEN

Look, I'm sure we can negotiate a reasonable—

KEEPER

(*Laughing*) You're so pitifully sad.

ALLEN

So that's it. I'm stuck in this hell hole with you. I have nothing . . . nothing left to negotiate with. Nothing that you want. Nothing that Henry wants.

KEEPER

(*Chuckling*) Oh, we're pretty sure Henry got what he wanted. (ALLEN *moans*) And what better place for you to end up really, than in your very own Land of Delete. Watch it!

Suddenly a tweet flies in. They both duck just in time as the tweet flies past and settles among the other images and messages at CENTER. They cross to Center to read the tweet.

KEEPER

Gosh. Our first tweet. We didn't even know tweets could be deleted!

ALLEN

What the heck? It's from my wife TO ME! (*Reading the tweet*) Cleaned up your mess dear Also learned valuable lesson Delete or be deleted Thanks #undeleted

KEEPER

Uh . . . now who's dumb as a rock?

ALLEN, *defeated, stares blankly, reaching for the headphones and pulling them off his ears. The cacophony of sound instantly fill the space.*

FADE TO BLACK.

Note

1 Depending on the theatre's technical budget and capabilities, the set and production elements for *Deleted* can be as simple or as elaborate as desired. Flying text, e-mail, tweet: This can be accomplished as simply as through the suggestion of the actors' ducking action and having the appropriate item pre-set; or by using paper airplanes for a humorous approach. The use of projections or other high tech is another option for theatres with the budget and equipment in place. Set options: The set can be elaborate with stacks of photos, messages and documents reaching into the fly space. On the other hand, a theatre wishing to simplify this production might create a suggestion of vertical stacks by utilizing three or four braced poles or planks of varying heights, covered with printed items and photographs, etc. A simple milk crate or two filled with file folders for the Keeper to sit upon will add to the suggestion that this place holds many types of deleted materials.

Chapter 8

Application of Guiding Questions to Pre-Production Phase

Deleted

Instructions

This exercise can be approached as either a theoretical application (you will work in isolation and consider the guiding questions as if working with a creative team) or as a practical application (you will be grouped with a creative team and stage manager to work through the guiding questions).

After reading the play *Deleted*, assume that you are in the Pre-production Phase of directing this production. As you prepare to face the creative team, you want to demonstrate your openness to discussion as well as your conviction and belief in your conceptual approach to the project. Review and apply the following guiding questions as you prepare *Deleted* for the initial production meeting. (Note: It may be difficult to do this work without fully researching and developing a concept. Please review the guiding questions in Chapter 6 as a basis for your work here.)

Parameters for the Exercise

Assume you are directing *Deleted* as part of a New Play festival for a small non-Equity theatre. You will be collaborating with a team of designers and will be assisted by a stage manager.

Director Considerations – Pre-Production Phase: Working with Your Creative Team for *Deleted*

1   Pre-Production Meetings

    a   In collaboration with the creative team, have you solidified your understanding of when and where *Deleted* takes place? The playwright offers latitude about the specific time of *Deleted*, while the place is well described, albeit non-real. Your decisions will influence all aspects of set, lights, and even costumes and props design discussions.

        • How will you present your overall concept of the play and ask for input/questions?

b   As each creative team is unique and each working environment organically forms in its own time, have you thought about your initial Forming, Storming, and Norming Stages for the creative team of *Deleted*? Being aware of how communication skills such as brainstorming, active listening, and questioning can ease your team through each stage and will go a long way toward creating a collaborative framework.

c   Have you clarified the mood of *Deleted*?

- How will you describe the play's atmosphere to the creative team?
- How will these elements be demonstrated in your overall concept?

d   This initial production meeting is a great opportunity for utilizing listening and questioning skills, demonstrating your openness to input from your entire creative team.

- Have you considered using photographs, music, clippings, video, or mementos to help illustrate your concept for *Deleted* and start a collaborative discussion?
- Have you brought in research samples, quotes, and articles to demonstrate your depth of research and preparation to help clarify the aesthetic emphasis of the play?
- Are you remaining open to the creative team's responses and allowing opportunities for questions, active listening, and brainstorming?

e   The sound design for *Deleted* is another major consideration, since it is important at both the beginning and end of the piece. Have you prepared notes and a list of questions before the first production meeting?

f   For your initial discussions with your set designer, have you prepared a simple sketch indicating any platforming or unit placement you may envision as part of your overall concept, and perhaps movement patterns? Understand that your sketch is simply a conversation starter, a starting point to allow the set designer to take this information and work his or her magic. A review of the playwright's production notes at the end of the script with your creative team is only meant to jump start brainstorming.

- Have you discussed your needs for function with the set designer? For instance, do both characters in *Deleted* need to sit on an object, or will only the Keeper be sitting?
- Depending on your concept for *Deleted*, there may be some technical challenges, such as tricky rigging in the way emails

and text messages are flown in. Be open to the set designer's and technical coordinator's suggestions and expertise in this area.

- Once the set design has been completed, have you reviewed the design to consider the safety of the actors as they interact with the set and asked questions?

By sharing your staging needs as well as your vision, a collaborative discussion with the set designer during the initial production meeting will produce a design that supports the overall concept and functions.

g   Depending on the specific concept you have settled on for *Deleted*, think about these questions as you prepare your pre-production meeting with the lighting designer:

- In what ways can lighting help to indicate *Deleted*'s world of deleted emails, texts, voicemails, and documents? The characters make reference to the space being "smaller than it looks." Can lighting help to create that illusion?
- In your concept, would this world be stark or colorful? The lighting designer will show you how lighting choices convey mood and atmosphere, best supporting the concept and vision you hope to communicate.

A discussion of lighting ideas during the initial production meeting helps to clarify the overall concept and will save time as tech draws near.

h   Have you considered how sound effects and incidental music can establish the desired mood and atmosphere for your *Deleted* concept? As mentioned above, the text does reference two important sound cues at the beginning and end of *Deleted*: a cacophony of sounds and noise. In addition to this signature sound element, consider the following:

- Are there other moments when sound may be appropriate and serve your concept for the production?
- In addition, have you considered incorporating pre- and post-show music for your production of *Deleted* as the audience enters/exits the auditorium, or would music be counterproductive to the overall concept?

Again, the sound designer will show you how sound and music choices can best support the concept and vision you are hoping to communicate to the audience.

i   The script has provided minimal costume suggestions for the two characters in *Deleted*. Allen is a businessman, wearing a three-piece suit. The Keeper of The Land of Delete is a young woman, wearing a one-piece jumpsuit, a white tee shirt, and a belt. There is a lot of leeway to use these descriptions as a base and connect more specifically to your concept for the play. Consider the following questions relating to your overall concept for *Deleted* and its effect on the costume design:

- Have you communicated the style and mood of the *Deleted*?
- What visual tools might you use (photos, magazine clippings, or rough sketches) to assist in the initial design meetings with the costume designer?
- What ideas for continued communication with the costume designer do you have while the actors in *Deleted* develop their characterization during rehearsals and ideas develop?

j If special effects will be used with your production of *Deleted*, there are several opportunities for collaboration. Consider the following:

- Often, the special effects coordinator and other designers work together to oversee the actual special effects device. If special effects will be used, will they be incorporated into the set, or become part of a prop or costume? This requires further collaboration with the set designer, props master, or costumer.
- Alternatively, would the special effect be enhanced if it was viewed through special lighting or coordinated with a sound effect? Therefore, further collaboration with the lighting or sound coordinator will be required.
- Have you considered actor safety when using a special effect? Be sure to seek the expertise of a trained specialist whenever actor safety is involved.

k There are a number of props used throughout *Deleted*. Some of these are simple hand props; others are actually rigged or part of the set design. Depending on your overall concept for your unique production of *Deleted*, consider the following:

- Have you thought about how your overall concept for *Deleted* will inform the prop master's selection or creation of props for this production?
- Does the prop master have a plan for enlarging the two photographs referred to by the Keeper? Is it even necessary for the photos to be large enough for the audience to see?
- How will you collaborate with the costumer and/or the actors to develop a list of possible character props? Specifically,

consider the headphones for Allen, as they must allow the actor to be able to hear clearly throughout the play.

- Have you thought of using a mini-brainstorming session to develop a list other character props?

Don't forget to refer to the Actor's Character Physical Analysis (see Appendix B), as character props often develop from these characterizations.

Have you thought about budgeting for each of the above production elements and challenges: set, lighting, sound, props, costumes, and special effects design?

Being open and listening to the creative team's advice may alter your initial thoughts and lead to new discoveries. Asking questions for clarification and encouraging input during the initial production meeting will demonstrate that you respect their expertise and will go a long way in creating a collaborative working environment.

Audition Requirements:

a   The Keeper in *Deleted* is described as "A funky young woman, who keeps track of affairs in The Land of Delete." This description leaves a lot of leeway for interpretation.

- How do you envision the character of the Keeper, and what will you look for in auditions? In contrast, how do you envision Allen as "an uptight, unscrupulous businessman"?
- How will you organize your auditions in terms of content, activities, and time for selecting the best actors for these roles and these requirements?

b   How will you briefly describe each of the characters in *Deleted* in advance of the auditions so that actors are fully aware what roles are available?

- How will your stage manager provide this information – as part of the audition posters, within a press release about the auditions, on social media, on a website, on a bulletin board at the theatre venue, or at the auditions?
- Can you and your stage manager collaborate on other ways to get the information out to interested actors?

Activities for Self-Reflection

Using your journal, respond to the following prompts based on your experiences as you work through a theoretical or practical approach to the Pre-Production Phase for a production of *Deleted*.

1 What have you discovered about the connection between a concept and the pre-production meetings with the design team?

2 In what ways have you attempted to inspire and motivate your creative team: by telling the story of the play, by challenging the team to participate in the concept, by letting them know you believe in them, by demonstrating your own enthusiasm for the project?

3 Describe the first audition you attended – as a director, actor, or stage manager. If you were the director of that audition today, describe one or two elements of the audition you might alter. Why?

4 Overall, what is your impression of the director's responsibility in collaborating with the creative team and stage manager during the Pre-production Phase of a production?

Chapter 9

Social Media Intermezzo 1.0
A Short Piece

Character Name	Brief Description	Age	Gender/Ethnicity
HUSBAND	A career professional, distracted	34	Male/Any
WIFE	A career professional, distracted	32	Female/Any
MAID	A professional, distracted	35	Either/Any
BABY (a doll)	Distracted	9 months	Either/Any

Social Media Intermezzo 1.0

by Jean Burgess

Scene: *Minimal scenery suggesting a breakfast room. A door frame at Center, with two briefcases placed at each side. At Right, a small round table with a single chair in the Down Right position and a baby's highchair opposite. At Left, a kitchen utility cart on wheels with a coffee maker and a toaster, suggesting a kitchen setting.*

The entire Intermezzo takes place with minimal speaking – a kind of staged choreography, perhaps to background music. The action should take place quickly and deliberately. It must be well-rehearsed, and timing must be impeccable.

LIGHTS UP

HUSBAND *enters from Right as* WIFE *enters from Left. They each carry a cellphone in their right hand and a cup of coffee in their left hand. They are both dressed in business suits, ready for work. They never take their eyes off their phones.* HUSBAND *and* WIFE *meet at Center and, without looking away from phones, give each other a quick kiss on the cheek.*

HUSBAND & WIFE

(*Simultaneously*) 'morning.

They each continue to cross to the opposite side of the stage.

HUSBAND *crosses to utility cart, sets down coffee cup and exits Left.* WIFE *crosses to table, sets down coffee cup and exits Right.*

MAID *enters from Left, carrying a baby (a doll can work just fine). The* MAID *has her nose in a phone and does not look up as she crosses to the highchair, places baby in the highchair, and props up an iPad that was lying on the highchair tray. She sits down in the chair Down Right.*

HUSBAND *enters from Left, eyes on his phone, picks up his briefcase from Left of the door, and crosses to highchair to kiss baby on the head.*

HUSBAND

'morning, sweetie.

He never takes his eyes off the phone. He crosses to the door and exits.

WIFE *enters from Right, eyes on her phone, picks up her briefcase from Right of the door, and crosses behind the table to* MAID, *kissing her on the head.*

MAID

Ick.

MAID and WIFE react at the mistake, briefly, then go right back to their phones. WIFE crosses to highchair and kisses baby on head.

WIFE

Bye bye, lovey.

She crosses to the door and exits.

MAID walks off Left, never taking her eyes off phone. BABY is left alone.

A long beat

The iPad falls down on the highchair tray. BABY lets out a huge wailing cry.

FADE TO BLACK.

Chapter 10

Application of Guiding Questions to Rehearsal Phase
Social Media Intermezzo 1.0

Instructions

Unlike the two previous plays, this short piece is written as a practical exercise. As a practical application, you will be grouped with a team of actors to work through the guiding questions.

Now that you have read *Social Media Intermezzo 1.0*, prepare to meet the actors in a lab setting. Consider how you will demonstrate your openness to discussion (listening, asking open-ended questions, brainstorming, if appropriate) as well as balance your belief in your conceptual approach to the project. While this piece is heavy in stage movement, there may be times in your directing career when you will be challenged with similar scripts, such as farces and physical comedies. For example, the second act of the comedy *Noises Off* is filled with timing-dependent movement and stage business, but very little dialogue. Guiding the ensemble to move together like a well-oiled machine without dictating blocking can be challenging.

For this exercise, try experimenting by having the actors run through the actions without inserting the minimal dialogue. Then return to the original version of the script and reinsert the dialogue. Experiment with pacing. Add music in the background. Ask the cast to submit a variety of musical genres with which to experiment. Discuss the differences these changes make with the cast.

Although *Social Media Intermezzo 1.0* is a short piece, practice following through with the early rehearsals, blocking rehearsals, refining rehearsals, and tech rehearsal format by reviewing and applying the following guiding questions. (Note: It may be difficult to do this work in isolation, without fully researching and developing a concept, even for a short scene. Please review the guiding questions in Chapter 6 as foundation for your work here.)

Parameters for the Exercise

Assume you are directing *Social Media Intermezzo 1.0* as part of an end-of-semester college lab assignment. As already stated, you are collaborating with peer actors on this directing project. As this is an educational project, you can assume royalties for the piece are waived.

Rehearsal Phase

1 Early Rehearsals

    a Even in the theatre lab environment, each cast are unique and each working environment organically forms in its own time. Consider the following:

- Have you thought about your initial Forming, Storming, and Norming Stages for the *Social Media Intermezzo 1.0* rehearsal process?
- Have you considered using an ice breaker or bonding exercise during the initial cast meeting?
- If you've considered incorporating physical and/or vocal warmups and trust activities to assist group bonding, which exercises would be most appropriate for the theatre lab environment as well as this particular piece?

    b Have you determined what type of table read is appropriate for *Social Media Intermezzo 1.0* – a single, quick read-through, or an extensive discussion of the play's theme and characters?

    c Have you set the tone for two-way discussion and open dialogue during the initial meeting in an effort to encourage a creative working environment?

    d Even as a lab exercise, developing an overall concept for *Social Media Intermezzo 1.0* will be beneficial. The introduction of your concept to the cast during the initial rehearsal is an important aspect of setting the stage for a creative working environment. Consider the following:

- How will you communicate your directorial concept of *Social Media Intermezzo 1.0* to the cast?
- Have you prepared a series of vivid words, a particular phrase, or a symbolic metaphor to help clarify your concept?
- Have you prepared visual tools, such as pictures, objects, magazine clippings, musical selections, or video clips to help express your ideas, if appropriate?

These activities will demonstrate that you are a disciplined, prepared director and will garner the respect of the cast while you introduce your version of the collaborative working environment.

    e How might your concept for the *Social Media Intermezzo 1.0* affect any choices the actors make concerning characterization?

f   As mentioned earlier in this guide, most professional actors will develop character backgrounds in their own time. For the sake of your lab exercise, have you encouraged the *Social Media Intermezzo 1.0* cast to use the Actor's Character Physical Analysis (see Appendix B) and the Actor's Character Background Analysis (see Appendix C) to aid them in examining the play for a physical and in-depth background characterization? These analyses are meant as a starting point for both discussion and rehearsal work.

2   Blocking Rehearsals

a   As mentioned in the opening scene description in *Social Media Intermezzo 1.0*, the action should to be quick and deliberate with impeccable timing. Have you thought about how you will aid the actors in developing this timing?

b   While sightlines may look great on paper, have you considered physically moving around the studio or auditorium throughout rehearsals to be sure all important moments are visible (and heard) from all seats in the house?

c   Have you broken down the use of props in *Social Media Intermezzo 1.0* as described in the text? Have you planned for a "business" rehearsal involving the use of cellphones, briefcases, coffee cups, etc.?

d   As the dialogue is minimal, the actors will be dependent on the script for movement more than dialogue. Have you considered ways to ease them off script?

3   Refining Rehearsals

a   Characterization – Are the actors' choices for characterization in synch with your overall conceptual vision for the play? What collaborative methods can you use as director to move the cast toward clarification?

b   Character relationships – What collaborative methods can you and the cast use to strengthen and define relationships between characters?

c   Scene rhythm and pacing exist even within a short play. There are natural rhythms present in *Social Media Intermezzo 1.0*. Your blocking and pacing decisions will be important. Consider the following questions:

• Have you identified moments that need to be highlighted, sped up, slowed down, or paused completely in *Social Media Intermezzo 1.0*? The lab environment is a great place to experiment with a willing cast.

- Are there other moments of silent beats that you might add in *Social Media Intermezzo 1.0* to communicate that which is not said verbally, but which speak volumes?

d Throughout the text we have explored the communication and leadership skills required to become a solid director in a creative collaborative environment. Consider the following rehearsal room skills:

- In what ways have you encouraged a two-way discussion with the cast as rehearsals have unfolded for *Social Media Intermezzo 1.0*?
- In what ways have you asked for input at appropriate moments throughout the process?
- What questions have you asked for clarification when a line, beat, or movement seems vague or unclear, and have you listened with a non-judgmental ear?
- How have you been open to adapting new ideas from a cast member about characterization, movement, and concept as rehearsals have progressed?
- Have you also had the courage to end a lingering discussion that has veered too far astray from your concept for *Social Media Intermezzo 1.0*?
- If you have set a goal for each rehearsal, how have you measured completion or success rate? Have you tried ending each rehearsal with a question as a motivator? Have you thanked the cast for their efforts at the end of each rehearsal?

4 Tech Rehearsal

a Have you collaborated with the creative team on a tech rehearsal plan for the performance of *Social Media Intermezzo 1.0*, to make the best use of actors' and tech crews' time, if appropriate for this exercise?

b Have you participated in a paper tech prior to the first tech with actors to pencil in light and sound cues with the stage manager, light designer, and sound designer, if applicable for this exercise?

c Have you laid the groundwork with the actors by reminding them of your changing focus during tech rehearsals, if applicable for this exercise?

d Have you taken the time during tech rehearsals to watch the performance of *Social Media Intermezzo 1.0* from the audience's point of view, asking yourself if the playwright's story is being obscured in any way by the production elements?

Activities for Self-Reflection

Using your journal, respond to the following prompts based on your experiences as you work through a practical application of the Rehearsal Phase for *Social Media Intermezzo 1.0.*

1   In which ways did you use the following communication skills with your cast?

> Open-ended questioning
> Active listening

2   Was there an opportunity to brainstorm at any point during this exercise? If so, describe how you incorporated brainstorming.
3   Did you observe the Forming, Storming, Norming, Performing group dynamics during this application exercise? If so, in what ways did you guide the cast through these group dynamics stages?
4   In what ways did you intentionally create a positive theatre environment for your cast during this exercise?

Part III

The Independent Project

Introduction

You are now ready to embark on your own collaborative directing project, whether an evening of ten-minute plays for a play festival, a youth theatre play at a Middle School, a local community theatre production, or a college lab play. Part I reviewed the qualities and characteristics a director needs to begin to create a positive collaborative theatre environment. You saw these concepts synthesized in the real-life example of the production *I Never Saw Another Butterfly* in an academic environment. Part II provided an opportunity for you to practice applying the guiding questions to three short scripts during the Preparation, Pre-production and Rehearsal Phases of production. The final section of this text broadens the range of guiding questions in the form of a checklist for you to apply to any independent directing project. The focus is on mastering your new skills in creating positive collaboration with the creative team and actors through each phase of your directing project.

Chapter 11

The Guiding Questions Checklist

This chapter presents an extensive list of guiding questions in a checklist format to use as you approach your next independent directing project.[1] During the Preparation Phase, the guiding questions focus on research and concept development, leading you to decisions around choosing the appropriate physical space for the production as well as planning for the audition process. The Pre-Production Phase deals with presenting your concept to the creative production team and collaborating on the design elements. Finally, the Rehearsal Phase highlights the early, blocking, refining, and tech rehearsals, and associated challenges. Examine each question and, if appropriate, check it off as you proceed through each phase of your directorial process.

Director Considerations – Preparation Phase

Initial Exploration

☐ Have you read the play several times, considering aesthetic/historical/cultural aspects, jotting down any key words, phrases, or images that resonate with you?

☐ Have you completed a thorough play analysis, including answering the following:

    ☐ Have you determined when and where the play takes place?

    ☐ Have you determined the play's general mood and/or atmosphere?

    ☐ Have you described the story are you telling and defined the conflict?

    ☐ Have you described the play's meaning in its own time, if a period piece?

    ☐ Have you determined the genre of the play?

    ☐ Have you described the world of the play and decided how you will be connecting the play to today's audience?

    ☐ Have you decided what the play's language suggests about the play?

☐ Have you determined if the play is Representational or Presentational, or both?

☐ Have you determined if the play is a period play and identified the period?

☐ Have you researched information about the playwright, other productions of the play, and reviews of those productions?

☐ Have you researched the time period of the play and/or the world of the play?

☐ Have you participated in field research?

☐ Can you state your initial concept of the play as a single word or phrase, or create a vivid image or metaphor?

☐ Once your overall concept is decided, have you considered how you will communicate this vision to both the creative team and the actors?

☐ Have you considered providing photographs, illustrations, sketches, even props and music, to help convey your concept at early production meetings and rehearsals?

☐ Have you evaluated the appropriateness of your concept for the production so that it does not impose on the playwright's intent?

Physical Space Considerations

☐ Have you considered which physical space might best suit the production of the play and your concept: proscenium, thrust, Theatre-in-the-Round, environmental, or some other experimental arrangement – to be discussed with the set designer?

☐ Have you considered the blocking and movement challenges that are associated with each choice of physical space?

☐ Have you reviewed character entrances/exits, placement of large groups, and audience sightlines?

☐ Have you determined if you will need to discuss certain arrangement of furniture or platforms with the set designer to accommodate blocking/movement needs?

☐ Have you created an initial sketch as a starting point for discussion with the set designer indicating entrances/exits and placement of required furniture or performance units?

☐ Have you used your sketch as a conversation starter to help articulate and list the minimal set requirements of your concept?

☐ If multiple scenes are required, have you prepared a sketch for each scene?

☐ Have you considered the technical production challenges associated with each physical space as well (i.e. lighting and set considerations are different with a thrust or in-the-round stage versus a proscenium stage)?

☐ If you are considering a unique theatre space (i.e. using the college student lounge or an outdoor venue), have you researched permission and necessary permits which may be required?

  ☐ Has your stage manager/production coordinator secured permission and dates before you publicize production meetings and rehearsals? (Note: This task may fall to you as director in some settings.)

Planning/Scheduling

☐ Has licensing been cleared and royalty been paid for the play you are about to direct? (Generally, this is the producer's responsibility for any play performed before a public audience, but this task may fall to you as director in some settings.)

☐ Have you determined how many weeks/number of hours of rehearsal are appropriate for a successful mounting of your play and collaborated with your stage manager to create a final rehearsal schedule?

☐ Have you considered the input of the creative team and production coordinator when planning for tech week rehearsals?

  ☐ Have you considered increasing tech rehearsals to perfect the timing of difficult tech transitions or tricky costume changes based on communication from the creative team?

☐ Have you considered including any special sessions (i.e. stage combat training, dialect coaching, choreography, movement specialist, or intimacy director) during rehearsals for the play, and have you allotted time in your rehearsal schedule for these consultants?

☐ Has your stage manager cleared all rehearsal spaces in advance of publishing the rehearsal schedule?

Director Considerations – Pre-Production Phase: Working with Your Creative Team

Pre-Production Meetings

☐ Have you communicated your understanding of when and where the play takes place and the mood/atmosphere of the play with the creative team?

  ☐ Have you clearly presented your overall concept of the play during the initial production meeting?

  ☐ Have you used photographs, music, clippings, video, and/or props to help illustrate your concept as well as to inspire the creative team?

☐   Have you brought in research samples, quotes, and articles to demonstrate your depth of research and preparation, and made these available to each designer on the creative team?

☐   Have you prepared a list of general questions to ask the creative team?

☐   Have you prepared notes and a list of questions before the first production meeting about the set requirements to begin discussions with the set designer?

☐   Have you considered how the style or historical time period of the concept you are presenting might affect the set design?

☐   Have you listened carefully to the set designer's initial suggestions about any technical challenges, such as tricky rigging, multiple set changes, or quick set changes/adjustments before asking questions?

☐   If a set piece or piece of furniture will be used in an unusual way, have you communicated that information to the set designer?

☐   Have you discussed the budget with the set designer?

☐   Have you prepared notes and a list of questions about the lighting needs for the production to discuss with the lighting designer?

☐   Have you listened carefully to the lighting designer's initial suggestions for lighting effects to convey the overall concept for this production before asking questions?

☐   Have lighting choices been coordinated with costuming?

☐   Have you discussed budget with your lighting designer?

☐   Have you prepared notes and a list of questions about the sound effects and incidental music that may serve the concept for the production?

☐   Have you listened carefully to the sound designer's initial suggestions for sound effects and incidental music for the production before asking questions?

☐   Have you considered if the production will be using recorded sounds or real sounds for best effect?

☐   Have you considered incorporating pre- and post-show music for the production as the audience enter/exit the auditorium?

☐   Have you discussed the budget with your sound designer?

☐   Have you made notes and a list of questions about the costumes that may serve the concept for the production?

☐   Have you listened carefully to the costume designer's initial suggestions for costuming for the production before asking questions?

☐   Have you communicated the historical period, if appropriate, as well as style and mood of the play as related to the concept?

☐   Have you discussed quick costume changes, if necessary?

☐   Have you communicated a plan for continued communication with the costume designer throughout the rehearsal process as the actors develop their characterization?

☐   Have you discussed the budget with your costume designer?

☐   Have you prepared notes and a list of questions about the use of special effects that may serve the overall concept for the production?

   ☐   Have you listened carefully to the special effects designer's initial suggestions for the production before asking questions?

   ☐   Have you considered if the production will use smoke, explosives, a pistol, etc., and if the creative team will need to collaborate to create any special effects into the production?

   ☐   Have you considered actor safety when using a special effect?

   ☐   Have you discussed the need for hiring a consultant to train actors on the use of special effect, if applicable?

   ☐   Have you discussed the budget with your special effects designer?

☐   Have you prepared notes and a list of questions about how your overall concept will inform the selection or creation of props for this production to review with the prop master?

   ☐   Have you listened carefully to the prop master's initial suggestions for the creation and/or use of props for the production before asking questions?

   ☐   Have you encouraged collaboration with the costume designer and/or the actors to develop a list of possible character hand props, including information resulting from the Actor's Character Physical Analysis (Appendix B), if appropriate?

   ☐   Have you considered using a mini-brainstorming session to develop this list of character props with the actors?

   ☐   Have you discussed which pieces of furniture and stage items, such as lamps, are practical?

   ☐   Have you discussed the budget with the prop master/designer?

Audition Requirements

☐   Have you determined how your conceptual approach to the production will affect the way you will conduct auditions?

   ☐   Have you decided how to organize your auditions in terms of time and content for the best results?

   ☐   Have you decided on using prepared monologues, scene readings, improvisations, or a combination as an audition vehicle for the style of production you are directing?

☐ Have you provided a brief description of each character in the play as well as a synopsis of the play to your stage manager to post with audition publicity? (Note: This task may fall to you as director in some settings.)

Director Considerations – Rehearsal Phase: Working with Your Actors

Early Rehearsals

☐ Have you considered incorporating an ice breaker, group warmups, and trust games into early rehearsals to help the cast bond?
☐ Have you decided how you will communicate your directorial concept/vision for the play to the cast to encourage collaboration as well as to inspire?

  ☐ Have you prepared vivid words/phrases, pictures/photos, objects, or music to clarify your concept's aesthetic/historical/cultural emphasis?
  ☐ Will you invite the creative team to present their designs during the initial rehearsal meeting, including set models, costume sketches, etc.?
  ☐ Have you considered how you will demonstrate the collaborative environment and tone you want to create at this initial rehearsal meeting?

☐ Have you determined the type and number of table reads appropriate for this project?
☐ Have you been mindful and open to a two-way discussion with your actors as rehearsals unfold?

  ☐ Have you asked questions of the actors to clarify your vision when a line or beat seems vague or unclear?
  ☐ Have you actively listened to the actors' input?
  ☐ Have you encouraged the actors' creative input and actively listened to their responses?
  ☐ Have you been willing to take risks that may seem uncomfortable at first?

☐ Have you considered encouraging the cast to explore the physical attributes and background of their characters by using tools such as the Actor's Character Physical Analysis (Appendix B) and Actor's Character Background Analysis (Appendix C), if appropriate?

Blocking Rehearsal

☐ Have you reviewed the text for ways to keep the action moving?

  ☐ Have you worked collaboratively with the actors to help them find appropriate actions or internal monologues?
  ☐ Have you asked questions about their characters to help motivate particular moments?

☐ Have you identified where there may be blocking challenges (i.e. fights, intimate moments, moments with lots of prop business, etc.)?

  ☐ Have you considered how you will handle each blocking challenge presented in the script?
  ☐ Have you determined where you might need to bring in a specialized consultant?
  ☐ Have you considered breaking down prop business into smaller parts or beats to help the actors work through the timing during rehearsals, if applicable?

Refining Rehearsal

☐ Have you reviewed the play for natural rhythms and emotional builds and determined how these will affect pacing?

  ☐ Have you identified these moments for rehearsal purposes?
  ☐ Have you and the cast identified these moments together?
  ☐ Have you watched the play from the audience's point of view, making sure the story is being clearly told?

☐ Have you worked collaboratively with the actors to explore the characters and their relationships within the world of the play during the refining rehearsals?

  ☐ Are the actors' choices for characterization in synch with the overall conceptual vision for the play?
  ☐ Have you found ways to stimulate experimentation with the cast on their Actor's Character Physical Analysis choices during in rehearsal, if applicable?
  ☐ Have you communicated and guided the actors to cohesive unity without obstructing their creative impulses?
  ☐ Are the character relationships clearly articulated?
  ☐ Have you considered incorporating improvisation to help your actors get to the core of their characters' intentions/objectives and relationships, if appropriate for this project?
  ☐ Have you found ways in rehearsal to discuss and ask questions about the casts' choices on their Actor's Character Background Analysis, if applicable?

Tech Rehearsal

☐ Have you collaborated with the production coordinator and/or the creative team on a tech rehearsal plan?

☐ Have you participated in a paper tech prior to the first tech with actors to pencil in light and sound cues with the stage manager, light designer, and sound designer?

☐ Have you laid the groundwork with the actors by reminding them of your changing focus during tech rehearsals?

☐ Have you taken the time during tech rehearsals to watch the performance from the audience's point of view, asking yourself if the playwright's story is being obscured in any way by the production elements?

Conclusion

By applying yourself to the exercises and activities presented throughout this guide, you have reflected on the kind of collaborative director you want to be. You understand the need for communication and leadership skills to build a foundation of respect and trust, and you know the amount of preparation and discipline involved to create and manage the collaborative working environment described. Continue to use this checklist of comprehensive guiding questions during your next several directing projects until these processes become second nature. Whether your next project occurs in the college theatre lab, a community theatre, a teen theatre at a local rec program, or a professional theatre, setting a goal of creating an inviting, collaborative working environment will only enhance the experience for you and your ensemble.

Note

1 This list of guiding questions is a compilation of directing "best practices" drawn from a cross section of directing resources as well as the author's forty-plus years of directing experiences. For example, see Michael Bloom's *Thinking Like a Director*, William Ball's *A Sense of Direction*, W. David Sievers, Harry E. Stiver, Jr., and Stanley Kahan's *Directing for the Theatre*, Frances Hodge and Michael McLain's *Play Directing: Analyses, Communication and Style*, and J. Michael Gillette's *Theatrical Design and Production: An Introduction to Scene Design and Construction, Lighting, Sound, Costume, and Makeup*, McGraw-Hill Higher Education, 2007.

Chapter 12

Concluding Thoughts

Congratulations! To those student directors who have applied themselves and worked through the reflective exercises throughout this guide, you've gained insight into yourself and the craft of collaborative stage directing. Asking yourself tough questions and spending time thoughtfully reflecting on your responses is a vital (and often overlooked) process at this point in your career. And self-discovery will go a long way in establishing yourself as a collaborative director as you consider the next steps in your directing journey.

Further, as you layered in the application exercises and began working with the guiding questions, you now have a better understanding of the stages of the directorial process. You see how preparation informs the pre-production work with your creative team, and how the pre-production collaboration creates a foundation for a smooth tech week. Additionally, your preparation frees you to work collaboratively, take creative risks, and allows open communication with your actors during the rehearsal phase.

You also realize that the role of collaborative director means mastery in coordinating, delegating, guiding, advising, empowering, participating and managing. You know that the road to a positive theatre environment is paved with compassionate leadership characteristics such as concern for actor safety, respect, positive attitude, free flow of ideas, and productivity. To maintain this atmosphere of excellence, you understand that communication skills, including questioning, active listening, and brainstorming, will guide you. Richard Pilchard, Baltimore School of the Arts teacher and director, offers:

> Listen, listen, listen. Respect everyone's input, and engage in dialogue, but at the end of the day, don't be afraid to make a decision. And – it's called a play for a reason, so play! If it ain't fun, why do it?

The most respected directors are those who demonstrate leadership, have found the balance between strength and collaboration, and always show respect to their casts and creative teams. As you incorporate motivational tools to inspire your ensemble, the example you set will go a long way to establishing a positive environment. Being attuned to both the actors' and creative team's creative processes and being willing to assess and quickly change direction are excellent motivators. You will find yourself moving away from using fear tactics and dictator-like stances, and moving toward encouragement and open, positive reinforcement.

If you have completed these exercises with passion and full intention, then you have created a solid foundation upon which to build your next directing credit, whether a classroom project, a resume-building career job, or even a recreational activity. You've become more mindful of the collaborative experience, with a balanced focus on process as well as presentation. Understanding how to create and manage a positive, creative working environment is key, where collaboration bests the individual ego and creativity excels for everyone. As we venture on to our next directing project, award-winning regional director and Tony-nominated theatre educator Donald Hicken beautifully reminds us:

> Be a good listener, respect your collaborators, remain humble, and remember that thorough and respectful artistic process is essential to a quality production. Individual ego is more likely to be an obstacle than an asset.

Developing a Production Concept

Approach #1: Random Ramblings

1) Read the play. Now read it again, and again, and again! Analyze the play for its aesthetic, historical and cultural aspects. Have a pad of paper nearby to record any thoughts or ideas that might jump out while you are reading. Don't censor these thoughts. Simply jot them down.

2) After several readings, review your random notes and see if any ideas, words, or phrases seem to resonate with you. Explore these for a possible overall production concept.

3) As mentioned earlier in the text, sometimes the play readings will evoke a single image or phrase, and this will be the seed of a concept that will be explored by the director and cast through the rehearsal process. As a word of caution, don't force a concept or impose a clever idea in the name of concept. In most cases, this approach becomes so heavy-handed that the true meaning of the play and often the playwright's very words become obscured. Your job is to discover a concept that will support the playwright's words. Finding balance is the duty of the director, and each reading will bring you closer to what truly resonates for you truthfully.

Approach #2: Historical-Cultural-Social-Political-Economic Imaging

1) Consider when and where the play takes place. If the playwright has provided a specific time and place in history, start doing some research and see if there are some significant cultural-social-political-economic issues or events that might inform that period of time. Explore the mood and tone of the time period.

2) For example, in researching the play A *Christmas Carol*, set in 1843, you may start by exploring the following:

- Cultural – the way Christmas is celebrated in 1843 England (i.e. customs, traditions, foods, etc.)
- Socio-economic – rich versus poorer classes; the problems facing the struggling classes in terms of housing, feeding, and clothing the family, medical attention, caring for the homeless and the hungry
- Political – laws and/or organizations in place to care for the poor and those who pushed back against this ideology

With each reading, continue to look for additional threads for research opportunities.

3) Look for essays, photos, videos, music, etc., and have these available at the initial production meeting and even the first rehearsal. This will go a long way in generating discussion, building a creative foundation, and inspiring excitement for the concept. Additionally, all of this information will add depth to your production and will help you communicate with both your actors and your creative staff.

Approach #3: Moving Ideas to Action

1) At times a director may find that the creative team grasp an abstract idea, while the actors respond better to action phrases. Understand that the designers will use the concept to guide their lighting, set, props, and costume work. The actors will use the concept to guide the development of their objective exploration, characterization, movement motivation, and more.

2) Table A.1 is an example of the process of moving random notes from the director's initial readings to a concept idea/phrase, and then from concept phrase to concept action. Using the play *I Never Saw Another Butterfly*, as described in Chapter 4, this is a partial listing of notes, concept ideas, and concept actions as well as possible design ideas and actor choices.

Table A.1 Process of moving notes to concept to action

Random Reading Notes	Concept Ideas	Concept Actions	Creative Team	Actor Choices
Butterfly symbol	Symbols of hate and hope	Searching for hope among the hate	Lighting idea: gobo of butterfly	Reaching out
Teaching hope			Set/prop idea: Colorful painting hung in dreary cinderblock room	Finding first love
Arts = hope	Paintings, songs poetry, opera			Slowly letting defenses down
Surrounded by hate			Set/props ideas: barbed wire fencing/suitcases and pile of shoes	
The darkness of hate	Nazi soldiers presence between scenes		Lighting idea: dark red scoops when soldiers enter	

Actor's Character Physical Analysis

Instructions

The director can provide this worksheet to actors in cases where a deeper analysis of physical attributes of the character is warranted. Encourage the actor to look for clues within the script: what does the playwright say about the character, what does the character say about herself/himself, and what do others say about the character.

Character Physical Analysis Worksheet

Your Name _____

Character Name _____

Physical

Age

Appearance

Walk

Any unusual habits (limp, flips hair, tics, etc)

Dress

Voice

Actor's Character Background Analysis

Instructions

The director can provide this worksheet to actors in cases where a deeper analysis of background and psychological attributes of the character is warranted. Encourage the actor to look for clues within the script: what does the playwright say about the character, what does the character say about herself/himself, and what do others say about the character.

Character Background Analysis Worksheet

Your Name   _____

Character Name   _____

Background

Family life

Education Level

Religious Attitudes

Political Attitudes

Career

Love Interest or Current Relationships

Hobbies

Psychological State

What do other characters say about the emotional state of your character? Be specific and cite examples from the script (continue on the back or a separate sheet if necessary).

What does your character say about his/her own emotional state? Be specific and cite examples from the script (continue on the back or a separate sheet if necessary).

Contributing Theatre Artists' Bios

Hamilton Clancy is Founding Artistic Director of The Drilling Company, home of Shakespeare in the Parking Lot in New York City since 1999, and partner with Bryant Park Corporation for Bryant Park Shakespeare since 2014. With The Drilling Company, Hamilton has commissioned and developed over 350 new plays, producing twenty-one projects over the past fifteen years celebrating playwrights of social conscience, including Brian Dykstra, P. Seth Bauer, Eric Henry Sanders, C. Denby Swanson, Trish Harnetiaux, Will Eno, and Vern Theissen. New York/ World Premiere directing credits include: *Over the Line* (P. Seth Bauer), *Mutant Sex Party* (Ed MacDonald), *Reservoir* (Eric Henry Sanders), *El Viaje de Beatrice* (Andrea Moon), *Bird Brain* (Vern Theissen), and *Wild Children* (Vincent Pastore).

Kate Danley is Co-Artistic Director of the Seattle Playwrights Salon. Kate directed and produced a monthly sketch show in Los Angeles, and her troupe appeared in the Los Angeles Comedy Festival as well as the Los Angeles Comedy Walk. She has been involved in theatre for over twenty-five years and was named a Maryland Distinguished Scholar in the Arts. She is a *USA Today* bestselling author and winner of the Panwoski Playwriting Award. Her plays have been produced internationally. She trained at The Groundlings, RADA, Towson University, and the Acme Comedy Theater.

Donald Hicken is Resident Director at The Annapolis Shakespeare Company and former Head of the Theatre Department at The Baltimore School for the Arts (thirty-seven years). Donald is an award-winning director and Tony finalist for Excellence in Theatre Education with over forty years of experience in professional theatre and conservatory actor training. His professional directing credits include productions at Everyman Theatre, The Annapolis Shakespeare Company, Center

Stage, The Round House Theatre, The Baltimore Shakespeare Festival, The Kenyon Festival Theatre, Pennsylvania Stage Company, and The Berkshire Theatre Festival. Donald was Head of the Theatre Department at The Baltimore School for the Arts (BSA) from its founding in 1979 to his retirement in 2016. At BSA he directed over fifty productions and developed local, regional, and international touring and outreach programs. In 2015 Donald was honored as one of two national finalists (out of a field of over 4,000 nominees) for the inaugural Tony Award for Excellence in Theatre Education.

Noah Himmelstein is Associate Artistic Director of Everyman Theatre, an Equity regional theatre in Baltimore, Maryland. Noah's professional directing credits include: *Los Otros*, *An Inspector Calls* (Everyman Theatre), Andrew Lipps' *I Am Anne Hutchinson/I Am Harvey Milk* (Music Center of Strathmore in Bethesda with Kristin Chenoweth – *Washington Post* Best of the Year), *The Forgotten Woman* (Bay Street Theatre, Sag Harbor), *Bleeding Love* (Fredericia Teater, Denmark), *I Am Harvey Milk* (Lincoln Center with Chenoweth, San Francisco's Nourse Theatre, Los Angeles' Disney Hall and Denver's Bellco Theatre – *NY & LA Magazine* Best of the Year, *Playbill* Unforgettable Experience of the Year), *Things I Left on Long Island* (Off-Broadway – *Time Out* New York Critic's Pick), *Positions 1956* (World Premiere Opera, Urban Arias), *Loving Leo* (Weston Playhouse), and *Great Writers Thank Their Lucky Stars* (DGF Gala with Stephen Sondheim and Bernadette Peters).

Dallas Munger is Founder of The Chalkboard Players in California's North Bay area. Dallas built this theatre in 2014 on a foundation of breaking down barriers to access to theatre for children and families in underprivileged areas. He has been involved in theatre for over twenty years, and has received awards for stage acting in the North Bay of San Francisco. He works as a Coordinator for Trauma Informed Arts Education, teaching visual and performing arts to children in schools and hosting a summer creative arts camps.

Richard Pilcher has been Principal Acting Teacher at Baltimore School for the Arts since the school began in 1981, as well as having taught acting and directing at Towson State University. Richard has acted on and Off–Broadway and in numerous resident theatres throughout the US. He has directed productions with the Baltimore School for the Arts and Towson University as well as the Utah Shakespeare Festival, and the Bay Theatre, among others.

Elizabeth van den Berg is Professor and Chair of Theatre Arts at McDaniel College in Westminster, Maryland, where she has directed over twenty productions. She serves as National Member at Large of the Kennedy Center American College Theatre Festival, and directed the Irene Ryan Showcase of Scenes at the Kennedy Center in 2016 and 2017. As a voice/dialect coach, Elizabeth has worked on over fifty productions in the DC area. She was awarded a Kennedy Center Gold Medallion in 2006 and again in 2015. In addition to the Voice and Speech Trainers Association, she is a proud member of Actors' Equity Association, SAG-AFTRA, Stage Directors and Choreographers, and a graduate of New York University's Grad Acting Program.

Building Your Library/Suggested Reading

Artaud, Antonin. *The Theater and Its Double*. 1938. Translated by Mary Caroline Richards. New York, Grove Press, 1994.

Ball, David. *Backwards and Forwards: A Technical Manual for Reading Plays*. Carbondale, IL, Southern Illinois University Press, 1983.

Ball, William. *A Sense of Direction: Some Observations of the Art of Directing*. New York, Drama Publishers, 1984.

Benedetti, Robert L. *The Director at Work*. New York, Prentice Hall, 1984.

Bloom, Michael. *Thinking Like a Director: A Practical Handbook*. New York, Farrar, Straus and Giroux, 2001.

Boal, Augusto. *Games for Actors and Non-Actors*. Translated by Adrian Jackson. New York, Routledge, 1992.

Bogart, Anne. *A Director Prepares: Seven Essays on Art and Theatre*. New York, Routledge, 2001.

Brecht, Bertolt. *Brecht on Theatre: The Development of an Aesthetic*. Translated by Steve Giles. New York, Farrar, Straus and Giroux, 1964.

Brook, Peter. *The Empty Space: A Book About The Theatre: Deadly, Holy, Rough Immediate*. 1968. New York, Touchstone, 1995.

Caird, John. *Theatre Craft: A Director's Practical Companion from A to Z*. New York, Farrar, Straus and Giroux, 2010.

Chandler, Wilma Marcus. *Directing Theatre 101: 10 Steps to Successful Productions*. Hanover, NH, Smith & Kraus, 2008.

Chinoy, Helen Krich and Toby Cole. *Directors on Directing: A Source Book for the Modern Theatre*. 1963. Berlin, Germany, Allegro Editions, 2013.

Clurman, Harold. *On Directing*. New York, Macmillan, 1972.

Cohen, Robert. *Working Together in Theatre: Collaboration and Leadership*. New York, Palgrave Macmillan, 2011.

Cohen, Robert and John Harrop. *Creative Play Direction*. 2nd ed., Englewood Cliffs, NJ, Prentice Hall, 1983.

Crook, Paul. *The Art and Practice of Directing for Theatre*. New York, Routledge, 2016.

Daniels, Rebecca. *Women Stage Directors Speak: Exploring the Influence of Gender on Their Work*. Jefferson, NC, McFarland, 1996.

Dean, Alexander and Lawrence Carra. *Fundamentals of Play Directing*. New York, Holt, Rinehart and Winston, 1974.

Eichenbaum, Rose. *The Director Within: Storytellers of Stage and Screen.* Middletown, CT, Wesleyan University Press, 2014.

Fliotsos, Anne. *American Women Stage Directors of the 20th Century.* Chicago, IL, University of Illinois Press, 2008.

Hauser, Frank and Russell Reich. *Notes on Directing: 130 Lessons in Leadership from the Director's Chair.* 2003. New York, Bloomsbury Publishing, 2008.

Hodge, Frances and Michael McLain. *Play Directing: Analyses, Communication and Style.* 7th ed., New York, Routledge, 2016.

Jory, Jon. *Tips: Ideas for Directors.* Hanover, NH, Smith & Kraus, 2002.

Knopf, Robert. *The Director as Collaborator.* New York, Routledge, 2016.

Knowles, Ric. *Fundamentals of Directing.* Toronto, Canada, Playwrights Canada Press, 2015.

Linklater, Kristen. *Freeing the Natural Voice.* New York, Drama Book Publishers, 1976.

Marowitz, Charles. *Directing the Action: Acting and Directing in the Contemporary Theatre.* New York, Applause Theatre and Cinema Books, 1991.

Mitchell, Katie. *The Director's Craft: A Handbook for the Theatre.* New York, Routledge, 2009.

O'Brien, Nick and Annie Sutten. *Theatre in Practice: A Student's Handbook.* New York, Routledge, 2013.

Robinson, Mary B. *Directing Plays, Directing People: A Collaborative Art.* Hanover, NH, Smith & Kraus, 2012.

Roznowski, Rob and Kirk Domer. *Collaboration in Theatre: A Practical Guide for Designers and Directors.* New York, Palgrave Macmillan, 2009.

Schechner, Richard. *Performance Theory.* 1977. New York, Routledge, 2003.

Schraft, Robin. *The Director's Toolkit: The Directing Process from Play Selection to Production.* New York, Routledge, 2018.

Shapiro, Mel. *A Director's Companion.* Scotts Valley, CA, CreateSpace Independent Publishing, 2018.

Sidiropoulou, Avra. *Directions for Directing: Theatre and Method.* New York, Routledge, 2019.

Sievers, W. David, Harry E. Stiver, Jr., and Stanley Kahan. *Directing for the Theatre.* 3rd ed., Dubuque, IA, Wm. C. Brown Co. Publishers, 1974.

Swain, Rob. *A Handbook for Emerging Theatre Directors.* London, Bloomsbury Publishing, 2011.

Wainstein, Michael. *Stage Directing: A Director's Itinerary.* Cambridge, MA, Hackett Publishing, 2012.

Index

Page numbers in **bold** refer to tables.